Java Precisely

Peter Sestoft

Java Precisely

The MIT Press
Cambridge, Massachusetts
London, England

This book was set in Times by the author using LATEX.

Printed and bound in the United States of America.

Library of Congress Cataloging-in-Publication Data

Sestoft, Peter.
  Java precisely / Peter Sestoft.
     p.   cm.
  Includes bibliographic references and index.
  ISBN 0-262-69276-7 (pbk. : alk. paper)
  1. Java (Computer program language) I. Title.

QA76.73.J38 S435 2002
005.13′3—dc21   2002016516

Contents

Preface   ix

Notational Conventions   ix

1 Running Java: Compilation, Loading, and Execution   2

2 Names and Reserved Names   2

3 Java Naming Conventions   2

4 Comments and Program Layout   2

5 Types   4
    5.1   Primitive Types 4
    5.2   Reference Types 4
    5.3   Array Types 4
    5.4   Subtypes and Compatibility 5
    5.5   Signatures and Subsumption 5

6 Variables, Parameters, Fields, and Scope   6
    6.1   Values Bound to Variables, Parameters, or Fields 6
    6.2   Variable Declarations 6
    6.3   Scope of Variables, Parameters, and Fields 6

7 Strings   8

8 Arrays   10
    8.1   Array Creation and Access 10
    8.2   Array Initializers 10
    8.3   Multidimensional Arrays 12
    8.4   The Utility Class Arrays 12

9 Classes   14
    9.1   Class Declarations and Class Bodies 14
    9.2   Top-Level Classes, Nested Classes, Member Classes, and Local Classes . . . 14
    9.3   Class Modifiers 14
    9.4   The Class Modifiers `public`, `final`, `abstract` 16
    9.5   Subclasses, Superclasses, Class Hierarchy, Inheritance, and Overriding . . . 16
    9.6   Field Declarations in Classes 18
    9.7   The Member Access Modifiers `private`, `protected`, `public` 18
    9.8   Method Declarations 20
    9.9   Constructor Declarations 22
    9.10 Initializer Blocks, Field Initializers, and Initializers 22
    9.11 Nested Classes, Member Classes, Local Classes, and Inner Classes 24
    9.12 Anonymous Classes 24

10 Classes and Objects in the Computer   **26**
    10.1   What Is a Class?   26
    10.2   What Is an Object?   26
    10.3   Inner Objects   26

11 Expressions   **28**
    11.1   Table of Expression Forms   28
    11.2   Arithmetic Operators   30
    11.3   Logical Operators   30
    11.4   Bitwise Operators and Shift Operators   30
    11.5   Assignment Expressions   32
    11.6   Conditional Expressions   32
    11.7   Object Creation Expressions   32
    11.8   Instance Test Expressions   32
    11.9   Field Access Expressions   34
    11.10 The Current Object Reference `this`   34
    11.11 Method Call Expressions   36
    11.12 Type Cast Expressions and Type Conversion   40

12 Statements   **41**
    12.1   Expression Statements   41
    12.2   Block Statements   41
    12.3   The Empty Statement   41
    12.4   Choice Statements   42
    12.5   Loop Statements   44
    12.6   Returns, Labeled Statements, Exits, and Exceptions   46
    12.7   The `assert` Statement   50

13 Interfaces   **52**
    13.1   Interface Declarations   52
    13.2   Classes Implementing Interfaces   52

14 Exceptions, Checked and Unchecked   **54**

15 Threads, Concurrent Execution, and Synchronization   **56**
    15.1   Threads and Concurrent Execution   56
    15.2   Locks and the `synchronized` Statement   58
    15.3   Operations on Threads   60

16 Compilation, Source Files, Class Names, and Class Files   **62**

17 Packages and Jar Files   **62**

18 Mathematical Functions   **64**

19 String Buffers   **66**

20 Collections and Maps   **68**
  20.1   The Collection Interface   70
  20.2   The List Interface and the LinkedList and ArrayList Implementations   71
  20.3   The Set Interface and the HashSet and LinkedHashSet Implementations   72
  20.4   The SortedSet Interface and the TreeSet Implementation   72
  20.5   The Map Interface and the HashMap Implementation   73
  20.6   The SortedMap Interface and the TreeMap Implementation   74
  20.7   Going Through a Collection: Iterator   76
  20.8   Equality, Comparison, and Hash Codes   76
  20.9   The Utility Class Collections   78
  20.10 Choosing the Right Collection Class or Map Class   80

21 Input and Output   **82**
  21.1   Creating Streams from Other Streams   83
  21.2   Kinds of Input and Output Methods   84
  21.3   Imports, Exceptions, Thread Safety   84
  21.4   Sequential Character Input: Readers   86
  21.5   Sequential Character Output: Writers   87
  21.6   Printing Primitive Data to a Character Stream: PrintWriter   88
  21.7   Reading Primitive Data from a Character Stream: StreamTokenizer   90
  21.8   Sequential Byte Input: InputStream   92
  21.9   Sequential Byte Output: OutputStream   93
  21.10 Binary Input-Output of Primitive Data: DataInput and DataOutput   94
  21.11 Serialization of Objects: ObjectInput and ObjectOutput   96
  21.12 Buffered Input and Output   98
  21.13 Random Access Files: RandomAccessFile   100
  21.14 Files, Directories, and File Descriptors   102
  21.15 Thread Communication: PipedInputStream and PipedOutputStream   102
  21.16 Socket Communication   104

References   **106**

Index   **107**

Preface

This book gives a concise description of the Java 2 programming language, versions 1.3 and 1.4. It is a quick reference for the reader who has already learned (or is learning) Java from a standard textbook and who wants to know the language in more detail. The book presents the entire Java programming language and essential parts of the class libraries: the collection classes and the input-output classes.

General rules are shown on left-hand pages mostly, and corresponding examples are shown on right-hand pages only. All examples are fragments of legal Java programs. The complete ready-to-run example programs are available from the book Web site <http://www.dina.kvl.dk/~sestoft/javaprecisely/>.

The book does not cover garbage collection, finalization and weak references, reflection, details of IEEE754 floating-point numbers, or Javadoc.

Acknowledgments Thanks to Rasmus Lund, Niels Hallenberg, Hans Henrik Løvengreen, Christian Gram, Jan Clausen, Anders Peter Ravn, Bruce Conrad, Brendan Humphreys, Hans Rischel and Ken Friis Larsen for their useful comments, suggestions, and corrections. Special thanks to Rasmus Lund for letting me adapt his collections diagram for this book. Thanks also to the Royal Veterinary and Agricultural University and the IT University of Copenhagen, Denmark, for their support.

Notational Conventions

Symbol	Meaning
v	Value of any type
x	Variable or parameter or field or array element
e	Expression
t	Type (primitive type or reference type)
s	Expression of type String
m	Method
f	Field
C	Class
E	Exception type
I	Interface
a	Expression or value of array type
i	Expression or value of integer type
o	Expression or value of object type
sig	Signature of method or constructor
p	Package
u	Expression or value of thread type

Java Precisely

1   Running Java: Compilation, Loading, and Execution

Before a Java program can be executed, it must be compiled and loaded. The compiler checks that the Java program is *legal:* that the program conforms to the Java syntax (grammar), that operators (such as +) are applied operands (such as 5 and x) of the correct type, and so on. If so, the compiler generates so-called *class files*. Execution then starts by loading the needed class files.

   Thus running a Java program involves three stages: *compilation* (checks that the program is well-formed), *loading* (loads and initializes classes), and *execution* (runs the program code).

2   Names and Reserved Names

A *legal name* (of a variable, method, field, parameter, class, interface or package) starts with a letter or dollar sign ($) or underscore (_), and continues with zero or more letters or dollar signs or underscores or digits (0–9). Avoid dollar signs in class names. Uppercase letters and lowercase letters are considered distinct. A legal name cannot be one of the following *reserved names:*

abstract	char	else	goto	long	public	synchronized	void
assert	class	extends	if	native	return	this	volatile
boolean	const	false	implements	new	short	throw	while
break	continue	final	import	null	static	throws	
byte	default	finally	instanceof	package	strictfp	transient	
case	do	float	int	private	super	true	
catch	double	for	interface	protected	switch	try	

3   Java Naming Conventions

The following naming conventions are often followed, although not enforced by Java:

- If a name is composed of several words, then each word (except possibly the first one) begins with an uppercase letter. Examples: `setLayout`, `addLayoutComponent`.

- Names of variables, fields, and methods begin with a lowercase letter. Examples: `vehicle`, `myVehicle`.

- Names of classes and interfaces begin with an uppercase letter. Examples: `Cube`, `ColorCube`.

- Named constants (that is, `final` variables and fields) are written entirely in uppercase, and the parts of composite names are separated by underscores (_). Examples: `CENTER`, `MAX_VALUE`.

- Package names are sequences of dot-separated lowercase names. Example: `java.awt.event`. For uniqueness, they are often prefixed with reverse domain names, as in `com.sun.xml.util`.

4   Comments and Program Layout

Comments have no effect on the execution of the program but may be inserted anywhere to help humans understand the program. There are two forms: one-line comments and delimited comments.

   Program layout has no effect on the computer's execution of the program but is used to help humans understand the structure of the program.

Example 1 Comments

```
class Comment {
  // This is a one-line comment; it extends to the end of the line.
  /* This is a delimited comment,
     extending over several lines.
  */
  int /* This delimited comment extends over part of a line */ x = 117;
}
```

Example 2 Recommended Program Layout Style
For reasons of space this layout style is not always followed in this book.

```
class Layout {                        // Class declaration
  int a;

  Layout(int a) {
    this.a = a;                       // One-line body
  }

  int sum(int b) {                    // Multi-line body
    if (a > 0) {                      // If statement
      return a + b;                   // Single statement
    } else if (a < 0) {               // Nested if-else, block statement
      int res = -a + b;
      return res * 117;
    } else { // a == 0                // Terminal else, block statement
      int sum = 0;
      for (int i=0; i<10; i++) {      // For loop
        sum += (b - i) * (b - i);
      }
      return sum;
    }
  }

  static boolean checkdate(int mth, int day) {
    int length;
    switch (mth) {                    // Switch statement
    case 2:                           // Single case
      length = 28; break;
    case 4: case 6: case 9: case 11:    // Multiple case
      length = 30; break;
    case 1: case 3: case 5: case 7: case 8: case 10: case 12:
      length = 31; break;
    default:
      return false;
    }
    return (day >= 1) && (day <= length);
  }
}
```

5   Types

A *type* is a set of values and operations on them. A type is either a primitive type or a reference type.

5.1   Primitive Types

A *primitive type* is either `boolean` or one of the *numeric types* `char`, `byte`, `short`, `int`, `long`, `float`, and `double`. The primitive types, example literals (that is, constants), size in bits (where 8 bits equals 1 byte), and value range, are shown in the following table:

Type	Kind	Example Literals	Size	Range
`boolean`	logical	`false`, `true`	1	
`char`	integer	`' '`, `'0'`, `'A'`, ...	16	`\u0000` ... `\uFFFF` (unsigned)
`byte`	integer	`0, 1, -1, 117,`...	8	$max = 127$
`short`	integer	`0, 1, -1, 117,`...	16	$max = 32767$
`int`	integer	`0, 1, -1, 117,`...	32	$max = 2147483647$
`long`	integer	`0L, 1L, -1L, 117L,`...	64	$max = 9223372036854775807$
`float`	floating-point	`-1.0f, 0.499f, 3E8f,`...	32	$\pm10^{-38}\ldots\pm10^{38}$, sigdig 6–7
`double`	floating-point	`-1.0, 0.499, 3E8,`...	64	$\pm10^{-308}\ldots\pm10^{308}$, sigdig 15–16

The integer types are exact within their range. They use signed 2's complement representation (except for `char`), so when the most positive number in a type is *max*, then the most negative number is $-max - 1$. The floating-point types are inexact and follow IEEE754, with the number of significant digits indicated by "sigdig." For character escape sequences such as `\u0000`, see page 8.

Integer literals (of type `byte`, `char`, `short`, `int`, or `long`) may be written in three different bases:

Notation	Base	Distinction	Example Integer Literals
Decimal	10	No leading `0`	`1234567890, 127, -127`
Octal	8	Leading `0`	`01234567, 0177, -0177`
Hexadecimal	16	Leading `0x`	`0xABCDEF0123, 0x7F, -0x7F`

For all primitive types there are corresponding wrapper classes (reference types), namely Boolean and Character as well as Byte, Short, Integer, Long, Float, and Double, where the last six have the common superclass Number. To use a primitive value, such as `17`, where an object is expected, use an object of its wrapper class, such as `new Integer(17)`.

5.2   Reference Types

A *reference type* is either a class type defined by a class declaration (section 9.1), or an interface type defined by an interface declaration (section 13.1), or an array type (section 5.3).

A value of reference type is either `null` or a reference to an object or array. The special value `null` denotes "no object." The literal `null`, denoting the null value, can have any reference type.

5.3   Array Types

An *array type* has the form `t[]`, where `t` is any type. An array type `t[]` is a reference type. Hence a value of array type `t[]` is either `null`, or is a reference to an array whose element type is precisely `t` (when `t` is a primitive type), or is a subtype of `t` (when `t` is a reference type).

5.4   Subtypes and Compatibility

A type t1 may be a *subtype* of a type t2, in which case t2 is a *supertype* of t1. Intuitively this means that any value v1 of type t1 can be used where a value of type t2 is expected. When t1 and t2 are reference types, t1 must provide at least the functionality (methods and fields) provided by t2. In particular, any value v1 of type t1 may be bound to a variable or field or parameter x2 of type t2, e.g., by the assignment x2 = v1 or by parameter passing. We also say that types t1 and t2 are *compatible*. The following rules determine when a type t1 is a subtype of a type t2:

- Every type is a subtype of itself.
- If t1 is a subtype of t2, and t2 is a subtype of t3, then t1 is a subtype of t3.
- char is a subtype of int, long, float, and double.
- byte is a subtype of short, int, long, float, and double.
- short is a subtype of int, long, float, and double.
- int is a subtype of long, float, and double.
- long is a subtype of float and double.
- float is a subtype of double.
- If t1 and t2 are classes, then t1 is a subtype of t2 if t1 is a subclass of t2.
- If t1 and t2 are interfaces, then t1 is a subtype of t2 if t1 is a subinterface of t2.
- If t1 is a class and t2 is an interface, then t1 is a subtype of t2 provided that t1 (is a subclass of a class that) implements t2 or implements a subinterface of t2.
- Array type t1[] is a subtype of array type t2[] if reference type t1 is a subtype of reference type t2.
- Any reference type t, including any array type, is also a subtype of predefined class Object.

No primitive type is a subtype of a reference type. No reference type is a subtype of a primitive type.

5.5   Signatures and Subsumption

A *signature* has form $m(t_1, \ldots, t_n)$, where m is a method or constructor name, and $(t_1, \ldots, t_n)$ is a list of types (example 25). When the method is declared in class T, and not inherited from a superclass, then its *extended signature* is $m(T, t_1, \ldots, t_n)$; this is used in method calls (section 11.11).

We say that a signature $sig_1 = m(t_1, \ldots, t_n)$ *subsumes* signature $sig_2 = m(u_1, \ldots, u_n)$ if each u_i is a subtype of t_i. We also say that sig_2 is *more specific* than sig_1. Note that the method name m and the number n of types must be the same in the two signatures. Since every type t_i is a subtype of itself, every signature subsumes itself. In a collection of signatures there may be one that is subsumed by all others; such a signature is called the *most specific* signature. Examples:

- m(double,double) subsumes itself and m(double,int) and m(int,double) and m(int,int).
- m(double,int) subsumes itself and m(int,int).
- m(int,double) subsumes itself and m(int,int).
- m(double,int) does not subsume m(int,double), nor the other way round.
- The collection m(double,int),m(int,int) has the most specific signature m(int,int).
- The collection m(double,int),m(int,double) has no most specific signature.

6   Variables, Parameters, Fields, and Scope

A *variable* is declared inside a method, constructor, initializer block, or block statement (section 12.2). The variable can be used only in that block statement (or method or constructor or initializer block), and only after its declaration.

A *parameter* is a special kind of variable: it is declared in the parameter list of a method or constructor, and is given a value when the method or constructor is called. The parameter can be used only in that method or constructor, and only after its declaration.

A *field* is declared inside a class, but not inside a method or constructor or initializer block of the class. It can be used anywhere in the class, also textually before its declaration.

6.1   Values Bound to Variables, Parameters, or Fields

A variable, parameter, or field of primitive type holds a *value* of that type, such as the boolean `false`, the integer `117`, or the floating-point number `1.7`. A variable, parameter, or field of reference type t either has the special value `null` or holds a reference to an object or array. If it is an object, then the class of that object must be t or a subclass of t.

6.2   Variable Declarations

The purpose of a variable is to hold a value during the execution of a block statement (or method or constructor or initializer block). A *variable-declaration* has one of the forms

> *variable-modifier type varname1, varname2, ... ;*
> *variable-modifier type varname1 = initializer1, ... ;*

A *variable-modifier* may be `final` or absent. If a variable is declared `final`, then it must be initialized or assigned at most once at run-time (exactly once if it is ever used): it is a *named constant*. However, if the variable has reference type, then the object or array pointed to by the variable may still be modified. A *variable initializer* may be an expression or an array initializer (section 8.2).

Execution of the variable declaration will reserve space for the variable, then evaluate the initializer, if any, and store the resulting value in the variable. Unlike a field, a variable is not given a default value when declared, but the compiler checks that it has been given a value before it is used.

6.3   Scope of Variables, Parameters, and Fields

The *scope* of a name is that part of the program in which the name is visible. The scope of a variable extends from just after its declaration to the end of the innermost enclosing block statement. The scope of a method or constructor parameter is the entire method or constructor body. For a control variable x declared in a `for` statement

> `for (int x = ...; ...; ...)` *body*

the scope is the entire `for` statement, including the header and the body.

Within the scope of a variable or parameter x, one cannot redeclare x. However, one may declare a variable x within the scope of a field x, thus *shadowing* the field. Hence the scope of a field x is the entire class, except where shadowed by a variable or parameter of the same name, and except for initializers preceding the field's declaration (section 9.1).

Example 3 Variable Declarations

```
public static void main(String[] args) {
  int a, b, c;
  int x = 1, y = 2, z = 3;
  int ratio = z/x;
  final double PI = 3.141592653589;
  boolean found = false;
  final int maxyz;
  if (z > y) maxyz = z; else maxyz = y;
}
```

Example 4 Scope of Fields, Parameters, and Variables
This program declares five variables or fields, all called x, and shows where each one is in scope (visible). The variables and fields are labeled #1, ..., #5 for reference.

```
class Scope {
  ...                 //
  void m1(int x) {    // Declaration of parameter x (#1)
    ...               // x #1 in scope
  }                   //
  ...                 //
  void m2(int v2) {   //
    ...               // x #5 in scope
  }                   //
  ...                 //
  void m3(int v3) {   //
    ...               // x #5 in scope
    int x;            // Declaration of variable x (#2)
    ...               // x #2 in scope
  }                   //
  ...                 //
  void m4(int v4) {   //
    ...               // x #5 in scope
    {                 //
      int x;          // Declaration of variable x (#3)
      ...             // x #3 in scope
    }                 //
    ...               // x #5 in scope
    {                 //
      int x;          // Declaration of variable x (#4)
      ...             // x #4 in scope
    }                 //
    ...               // x #5 in scope
  }                   //
  ...                 //
  int x;              // Declaration of field x (#5)
  ...                 // x #5 in scope
}
```

7   Strings

A *string* is an object of the predefined class String. A string literal is a sequence of characters within double quotes: "New York", "A38", "", and so on. Internally, a character is stored as a number using the Unicode character encoding, whose character codes 0–127 coincide with the old ASCII character encoding. String literals and character literals may use character *escape sequences*:

Escape Code	Meaning
\b	backspace
\t	horizontal tab
\n	newline
\f	form feed (page break)
\r	carriage return
\"	the double quote character
\'	the single quote character
\\	the backslash character
ddd	the character whose character code is the three-digit octal number *ddd*
\u*dddd*	the character whose character code is the four-digit hexadecimal number *dddd*

A character escape sequence represents a single character. Since the letter A has code 65 (decimal), which is written 101 in octal and 0041 in hexadecimal, the string literal "A\101\u0041" is the same as "AAA". If s1 and s2 are expressions of type String and v is an expression of any type, then

- s1.length() of type int is the length of s1, that is, the number of characters in s1.

- s1.equals(s2) of type boolean is true if s1 and s2 contain the same sequence of characters, and false otherwise; equalsIgnoreCase is similar but does not distinguish lowercase and uppercase.

- s1.charAt(i) of type char is the character at position i in s1, counting from 0. If the index i is less than 0, or greater than or equal to s1.length(), then StringIndexOutOfBoundsException is thrown.

- s1.toString() of type String is the same object as s1.

- String.valueOf(v) returns the string representation of v, which can have any primitive type (section 5.1) or reference type. When v has reference type and is not null, then it is converted using v.toString(); if it is null, then it is converted to the string "null". Any class C inherits from Object a default toString method that produces strings of the form C@2a5734, where 2a5734 is some memory address, but toString may be overridden to produce more useful strings.

- s1 + s2 has the same meaning as s1.concat(s2): it constructs the concatenation of s1 and s2, a new String consisting of the characters of s1 followed by the characters of s2.

- s1 + v and v + s1 are evaluated by converting v to a string with String.valueOf(v), thus using v.toString() when v has reference type, and then concatenating the resulting strings.

- s1.compareTo(s2) returns a negative integer, zero, or a positive integer, according as s1 precedes, equals, or follows s2 in the usual lexicographical ordering based on the Unicode character encoding. If s1 or s2 is null, then the exception NullPointerException is thrown. Method compareToIgnoreCase is similar but does not distinguish lowercase and uppercase.

- More String methods are described in the Java class library documentation [3].

Example 5 Equality of Strings, and the Subtlety of the (+) Operator

```
String s1 = "abc";
String s2 = s1 + "";        // New object, but contains same text as s1
String s3 = s1;             // Same object as s1
String s4 = s1.toString();  // Same object as s1
// The following statements print false, true, true, true, true:
System.out.println("s1 and s2 identical objects: " + (s1 == s2));
System.out.println("s1 and s3 identical objects: " + (s1 == s3));
System.out.println("s1 and s4 identical objects: " + (s1 == s4));
System.out.println("s1 and s2 contain same text: " + (s1.equals(s2)));
System.out.println("s1 and s3 contain same text: " + (s1.equals(s3)));
// These two statements print 35A and A1025 because (+) is left-associative:
System.out.println(10 + 25 + "A");  // Same as (10 + 25) + "A"
System.out.println("A" + 10 + 25);  // Same as ("A" + 10) + 25
```

Example 6 Concatenating All Command Line Arguments
When concatenating many strings, use a string buffer instead (chapter 19 and example 84).

```
public static void main(String[] args) {
  String res = "";
  for (int i=0; i<args.length; i++)
    res += args[i];
  System.out.println(res);
}
```

Example 7 Counting the Number of e's in a String

```
static int ecount(String s) {
  int ecount = 0;
  for (int i=0; i<s.length(); i++)
    if (s.charAt(i) == 'e')
      ecount++;
  return ecount;
}
```

Example 8 Determining Whether Strings Occur in Lexicographically Increasing Order

```
static boolean sorted(String[] a) {
  for (int i=1; i<a.length; i++)
    if (a[i-1].compareTo(a[i]) > 0)
      return false;
  return true;
}
```

Example 9 Using a Class That Declares a toString Method
The class Point (example 16) declares a toString method that returns a string of the point coordinates. The operator (+) calls the toString method implicitly to format the Point objects.

```
Point p1 = new Point(10, 20), Point p2 = new Point(30, 40);
System.out.println("p1 is " + p1);      // Prints: p1 is (10, 20)
System.out.println("p2 is " + p2);      // Prints: p2 is (30, 40)
p2.move(7, 7);
System.out.println("p2 is " + p2);      // Prints: p2 is (37, 47)
```

8   Arrays

An *array* is an indexed collection of variables, called *elements*. An array has a given *length* $\ell \geq 0$ and a given *element type* t. The elements are indexed by the integers $0, 1, \ldots, \ell - 1$. The value of an expression of array type u[] is either null or a reference to an array whose element type t is a subtype of u. If u is a primitive type, then t must equal u.

8.1   Array Creation and Access

A new array of length ℓ with element type t is created (allocated) using an *array creation expression*:

```
new t[ℓ]
```

where ℓ is an expression of type int. If type t is a primitive type, all elements of the new array are initialized to 0 (when t is byte, char, short, int, or long) or 0.0 (when t is float or double) or false (when t is boolean). If t is a reference type, all elements are initialized to null.

If ℓ is negative, then the exception NegativeArraySizeException is thrown.

Let a be a reference of array type u[], to an array with length ℓ and element type t. Then

- a.length of type int is the length ℓ of a, that is, the number of elements in a.

- The *array access* expression a[i] denotes element number i of a, counting from 0; this expression has type u. The integer expression i is called the *array index*. If the value of i is less than 0 or greater than or equal to a.length, then exception ArrayIndexOutOfBoundsException is thrown.

- When t is a reference type, every array element assignment a[i] = e checks that the value of e is null or a reference to an object whose class C is a subtype of the element type t. If this is not the case, then the exception ArrayStoreException is thrown. This check is made before every array element assignment at run-time, but only for reference types.

8.2   Array Initializers

A variable or field of array type may be initialized at declaration, using an existing array or an *array initializer* for the initial value. An array initializer is a comma-separated list of zero or more expressions enclosed in braces { ... }:

```
t[] x = { expression, ..., expression }
```

The type of each *expression* must be a subtype of t. Evaluation of the initializer causes a distinct new array, whose length equals the number of expressions, to be allocated. Then the expressions are evaluated from left to right and their values are stored in the array, and finally the array is bound to x. Hence x cannot occur in the *expressions:* it has not been initialized when they are evaluated.

Array initializers may also be used in connection with array creation expressions:

```
new t[] { expression, ..., expression }
```

Multidimensional arrays can have nested initializers (example 14). Note that there are no array constants: a new distinct array is created every time an array initializer is evaluated.

Example 10 Creating and Using One-Dimensional Arrays
The first half of this example rolls a die one thousand times, then prints the frequencies of the outcomes. The second half creates and initializes an array of String objects.

```
int[] freq = new int[6];                 // All initialized to 0
for (int i=0; i<1000; i++) {             // Roll dice, count frequencies
  int die = (int)(1 + 6 * Math.random());
  freq[die-1] += 1;
}
for (int c=1; c<=6; c++)
  System.out.println(c + " came up " + freq[c-1] + " times");

String[] number = new String[20];        // Create array of null elements
for (int i=0; i<number.length; i++)      // Fill with strings "A0", ..., "A19"
  number[i] = "A" + i;
for (int i=0; i<number.length; i++)      // Print strings
  System.out.println(number[i]);
```

Example 11 Array Element Assignment Type Check at Run-Time
This program compiles, but at run-time a[2]=d throws ArrayStoreException, since the class of the object bound to d (that is, Double) is not a subtype of a's element type (that is, Integer).

```
Number[] a = new Integer[10];      // Length 10, element type Integer
Double d = new Double(3.14);       // Type Double,  class Double
Integer i = new Integer(117);      // Type Integer, class Integer
Number n = i;                      // Type Number,  class Integer
a[0] = i;                          // OK, Integer is subtype of Integer
a[1] = n;                          // OK, Integer is subtype of Integer
a[2] = d;                          // No, Double not subtype of Integer
```

Example 12 Using an Initialized Array
Method checkdate here behaves the same as checkdate in example 2. The array should be declared outside the method, otherwise a distinct new array is created for every call to the method.

```
static int[] days = { 31, 28, 31, 30, 31, 30, 31, 31, 30, 31, 30, 31 };
static boolean checkdate(int mth, int day)
{ return (mth >= 1) && (mth <= 12) && (day >= 1) && (day <= days[mth-1]); }
```

Example 13 Creating a String from a Character Array
When replacing character c1 by character c2 in a string, the result can be built in a character array because its length is known. This is 50 percent faster than example 85 which uses a string buffer.

```
static String replaceCharChar(String s, char c1, char c2) {
  char[] res = new char[s.length()];
  for (int i=0; i<s.length(); i++)
    if (s.charAt(i) == c1)
      res[i] = c2;
    else
      res[i] = s.charAt(i);
  return new String(res);          // A string containing the characters of res
}
```

8.3   Multidimensional Arrays

The types of multidimensional arrays are written t[][], t[][][], and so on. A rectangular n-dimensional array of size $\ell_1 \times \ell_2 \times \cdots \times \ell_n$ is created (allocated) using the array creation expression

   new t[ℓ_1][ℓ_2]...[ℓ_n]

A multidimensional array a of type t[][] is in fact a one-dimensional array of arrays; its component arrays have type t[]. Hence a multidimensional array need not be rectangular, and one need not create all the dimensions at once. To create only the first k dimensions of size $\ell_1 \times \ell_2 \times \cdots \times \ell_k$ of an n-dimensional array, leave the $(n-k)$ last brackets empty:

   new t[ℓ_1][ℓ_2]...[ℓ_k][]...[]

To access an element of an n-dimensional array a, use n index expressions: a[i_1][i_2]...[i_n].

8.4   The Utility Class Arrays

Class Arrays from package java.util provides static utility methods to compare, fill, sort, and search arrays, and to create a collection (chapter 20) from an array. The binarySearch, equals, fill, and sort methods are overloaded also on arrays of type byte, char, short, int, long, float, double, Object; and equals and fill also on type boolean. The Object versions of binarySearch and sort use the compareTo method of the array elements, unless an explicit Comparator object (section 20.8) is given.

- static List asList(Object[] a) returns a java.util.List view of the elements of a, in index order. The resulting list implements RandomAccess (section 20.2 and example 94).
- static int binarySearch(byte[] a, byte k) returns an index i>=0 for which a[i]==k, if any; otherwise returns i<0 such that (-i-1) would be the proper position for k. The array a must be sorted, as by sort(a), or else the result is undefined.
- static int binarySearch(Object[] a, Object k) works like the preceding method, but compares array elements using their compareTo method (section 20.8 and example 94).
- static int binarySearch(Object[] a, Object k, Comparator cmp) works like the preceding method, but compares array elements using the method cmp.compare (section 20.8).
- static boolean equals(byte[] a1, byte[] a2) returns true if a1 and a2 have the same length and contain the same elements, in the same order.
- static boolean equals(Object[] a1, Object[] a2) works like the preceding method, but compares array elements using their equals method (section 20.8).
- static void fill(byte[] a, byte v) sets all elements of a to v.
- static void fill(byte[] a, int from, int to, byte v) sets a[from..(to-1)] to v.
- static void sort(byte[] a) sorts the array a using quicksort.
- static void sort(Object[] a) sorts the array a using mergesort, comparing array elements using their compareTo method (section 20.8).
- static void sort(Object[] a, Comparator cmp) works like the preceding method, but compares array elements using the method cmp.compare (section 20.8).
- static void sort(byte[] a, int from, int to) sorts a[from..(to-1)].

Example 14 Creating Multidimensional Arrays

Consider this rectangular 3-by-2 array and this two-dimensional "jagged" (lower triangular) array:

```
0.0   0.0              0.0
0.0   0.0              0.0   0.0
0.0   0.0              0.0   0.0   0.0
```

The following program shows two ways (r1, r2) to create the rectangular array, and three ways (t1, t2, t3) to create the "jagged" array:

```
double[][] r1 = new double[3][2];
double[][] r2 = new double[3][];
for (int i=0; i<3; i++)
  r2[i] = new double[2];

double[][] t1 = new double[3][];
for (int i=0; i<3; i++)
  t1[i] = new double[i+1];
double[][] t2 = { { 0.0 }, { 0.0, 0.0 }, { 0.0, 0.0, 0.0 } };
double[][] t3 = new double[][] { { 0.0 }, { 0.0, 0.0 }, { 0.0, 0.0, 0.0 } };
```

Example 15 Using Multidimensional Arrays

The genetic material of living organisms is held in DNA, conceptually a string AGCTTTTCA of nucleotides A, C, G, and T. A triple of nucleotides, such as AGC, is called a codon; a codon may code for an amino acid. This program counts the frequencies of the $4 \cdot 4 \cdot 4 = 64$ possible codons, using a three-dimensional array freq. The auxiliary array fromNuc translates from the nucleotide letters (A,C,G,T) to the indexes (0,1,2,3) used in freq. The array toNuc translates from indexes to nucleotide letters when printing the frequencies.

```
static void codonfreq(String s) {
  int[] fromNuc = new int[128];
  for (int i=0; i<fromNuc.length; i++)
    fromNuc[i] = -1;
  fromNuc['a'] = fromNuc['A'] = 0; fromNuc['c'] = fromNuc['C'] = 1;
  fromNuc['g'] = fromNuc['G'] = 2; fromNuc['t'] = fromNuc['T'] = 3;
  int[][][] freq = new int[4][4][4];
  for (int i=0; i+2<s.length(); i+=3) {
    int nuc1 = fromNuc[s.charAt(i)];
    int nuc2 = fromNuc[s.charAt(i+1)];
    int nuc3 = fromNuc[s.charAt(i+2)];
    freq[nuc1][nuc2][nuc3] += 1;
  }
  final char[] toNuc = { 'A', 'C', 'G', 'T' };
  for (int i=0; i<4; i++)
    for (int j=0; j<4; j++) {
      for (int k=0; k<4; k++)
        System.out.print(" "+toNuc[i]+toNuc[j]+toNuc[k]+": " + freq[i][j][k]);
      System.out.println();
    }
}
```

9   Classes

9.1   Class Declarations and Class Bodies

A *class-declaration* of class C has the form

> *class-modifiers* class C *extends-clause implements-clause*
>   *class-body*

A declaration of class C introduces a new reference type C. The *class-body* may contain declarations of fields, constructors, methods, nested classes, nested interfaces, and initializer blocks. The declarations in a class may appear in any order:

> {
>   *field-declarations*
>   *constructor-declarations*
>   *method-declarations*
>   *class-declarations*
>   *interface-declarations*
>   *initializer-blocks*
> }

A field, method, nested class, or nested interface is called a *member* of the class. A member may be declared static. A nonstatic member is also called an *instance member*.

The scope of a member is the entire class body, except where shadowed by a variable or parameter or by a member of a nested class or interface. The scope of a (static) field does not include (static) initializers preceding its declaration, but the scope of a static field does include all nonstatic initializers. There can be no two nested classes or interfaces with the same name, and no two fields with the same name, but a field, a method and a class (or interface) may have the same name.

By *static code* we mean expressions and statements in static field initializers, static initializer blocks, and static methods. By *nonstatic code* we mean expressions and statements in constructors, nonstatic field initializers, nonstatic initializer blocks, and nonstatic methods. Nonstatic code is executed inside a *current object*, which can be referred to as this (section 11.10). Static code cannot refer to nonstatic members or to this, only to static members.

9.2   Top-Level Classes, Nested Classes, Member Classes, and Local Classes

A *top-level class* is a class declared outside any other class or interface declaration. A *nested class* is a class declared inside another class or interface. There are two kinds of nested classes: a *local class* is declared inside a method or constructor or initializer block; a *member class* is not. A nonstatic member class, or a local class in a nonstatic member, is called an *inner class*, because an object of the inner class will contain a reference to an object of the enclosing class. See also section 9.11.

9.3   Class Modifiers

For a top-level class, the *class-modifiers* may be a list of public and at most one of abstract and final. For a member class, the *class-modifiers* may be a list of static, and at most one of abstract and final, and at most one of private, protected, and public. For a local class, the *class-modifiers* may be at most one of abstract and final.

Example 16 Class Declaration
The Point class is declared to have two nonstatic fields x and y, one constructor, and two nonstatic methods. It is used in example 41.

```
class Point {
  int x, y;

  Point(int x, int y) { this.x = x; this.y = y; }

  void move(int dx, int dy) { x += dx; y += dy; }

  public String toString() { return "(" + x + ", " + y + ")"; }
}
```

Example 17 Class with Static and Nonstatic Members
The SPoint class declares a static field `allpoints` and two nonstatic fields x and y. Thus each SPoint object has its own x and y fields, but all objects share the same `allpoints` field in the SPoint class.

   The constructor inserts the new object (`this`) into the ArrayList object `allpoints` (section 20.2). The nonstatic method `getIndex` returns the point's index in the array list. The static method `getSize` returns the number of SPoints created so far. The static method `getPoint` returns the i'th SPoint in the array list. Class SPoint is used in example 48.

```
class SPoint {
  static ArrayList allpoints = new ArrayList();
  int x, y;

  SPoint(int x, int y) { allpoints.add(this); this.x = x; this.y = y; }
  void move(int dx, int dy) { x += dx; y += dy; }
  public String toString() { return "(" + x + ", " + y + ")"; }
  int getIndex() { return allpoints.indexOf(this); }
  static int getSize() { return allpoints.size(); }
  static SPoint getPoint(int i) { return (SPoint)allpoints.get(i); }
}
```

Example 18 Top-Level, Member, and Local Classes
See also examples 31 and 36.

```
class TLC {                        // Top-level class TLC
  static class SMC { ... }         // Static member class

  class NMC { ... }                // Nonstatic member (inner) class

  void nm() {                      // Nonstatic method in TLC
    class NLC { ... }              // Local (inner) class in method
  }

  static void sm() {               // Static method in TLC
    class SLC { ... }              // Local class in method
  }
}
```

9.4   The Class Modifiers `public`, `final`, `abstract`

If a top-level class C is declared `public`, then it is accessible outside its package (chapter 17).

If a class C is declared `final`, one cannot declare subclasses of C and hence cannot override any methods declared in C. This is useful for preventing rogue subclasses from violating data representation invariants.

If a class C is declared `abstract`, then it cannot be instantiated, but nonabstract subclasses of C can be instantiated. An abstract class may declare constructors and have initializers, to be executed when instantiating nonabstract subclasses. An abstract class may declare abstract and nonabstract methods; a nonabstract class cannot declare abstract methods. A class cannot be both `abstract` and `final`, because no objects could be created of that class.

9.5   Subclasses, Superclasses, Class Hierarchy, Inheritance, and Overriding

A class C may be declared as a *subclass* of class B by an *extends-clause* of the form

```
class C extends B { ... }
```

In this case, C is a subclass and hence a subtype (section 5.4) of B and its supertypes. Class C inherits all methods and fields (even private ones, although they are not accessible in class C), but not the constructors, from B.

Class B is called the *immediate superclass* of C. A class can have at most one immediate superclass. The predefined class Object is a superclass of all other classes; class Object has no superclass. Hence the classes form a *class hierarchy* in which every class is a descendant of its immediate superclass, except Object, which is at the top.

To perform some initialization, a constructor in subclass C may, as its very first action, explicitly call a constructor in the immediate superclass B, using this syntax:

```
super(actual-list);
```

A superclass constructor call `super(...)` may appear only at the very beginning of a constructor.

If a constructor C(...) in subclass C does not explicitly call `super(...)` as its first action, then it implicitly calls the argumentless *default constructor* B() in superclass B as its first action, as if by `super()`. In this case, B must have a nonprivate argumentless constructor B(). Conversely, if there is no argumentless constructor B() in B, then C(...) in C must use `super(...)` to explicitly call some other constructor in B.

The declaration of C may *override* (redeclare) any nonfinal method m inherited from B by declaring a new method m with the exact same signature. An overridden B-method m can be referred to as `super.m` inside C's constructors, nonstatic methods, and nonstatic initializers.

The overriding method m in C

- must be at least as accessible (section 9.7) as the overridden method in B;
- must have the same signature and return type as the overridden method in B;
- must be static if and only if the overridden method in B is static;
- either has no *throws-clause*, or has a *throws-clause* that covers no more exception classes than the *throws-clause* (if any) of the overridden method in B.

However, the declaration of a class C cannot redeclare a field f inherited from B, but only declare an additional field of the same name (section 9.6). The overridden B-field can be referred to as `super.f` inside C's constructors, nonstatic methods, and nonstatic initializers.

Example 19 Abstract Classes, Subclasses, and Overriding
The abstract class Vessel models the notion of a vessel (for holding liquids): it has a field contents representing its actual contents, an abstract method capacity for computing its maximal capacity, and a method for
filling in more, but only up to its capacity (the excess will be lost). The abstract class has subclasses Tank (a
rectangular vessel), Cube (a cubic vessel, subclass of Tank), and Barrel (a cylindrical vessel).

The subclasses implement the capacity method, they inherit the contents field and the fill method
from the superclass, and they override the toString method (inherited from class Object) to print each vessel
object appropriately.

```
abstract class Vessel {
  double contents;
  abstract double capacity();
  void fill(double amount) { contents = Math.min(contents + amount, capacity()); }
}
class Tank extends Vessel {
  double length, width, height;
  Tank(double length, double width, double height)
  { this.length = length; this.width = width; this.height = height; }
  double capacity() { return length * width * height; }
  public String toString()
  { return "tank (" + length + ", " + width + ", " + height + ")"; }
}
class Cube extends Tank {
  Cube(double side) { super(side, side, side); }
  public String toString() { return "cube (" + length + ")"; }
}
class Barrel extends Vessel {
  double radius, height;
  Barrel(double radius, double height) { this.radius = radius; this.height = height; }
  double capacity() { return height * Math.PI * radius * radius; }
  public String toString() { return "barrel (" + radius + ", " + height + ")"; }
}
```

Example 20 Using the Vessel Hierarchy from Example 19
The call vs[i].capacity() is legal only because the method capacity, although abstract, is declared in
class Vessel (example 19):

```
public static void main(String[] args) {
  Vessel v1 = new Barrel(3, 10);
  Vessel v2 = new Tank(10, 20, 12);
  Vessel v3 = new Cube(4);
  Vessel[] vs = { v1, v2, v3 };
  v1.fill(90); v1.fill(10); v2.fill(100); v3.fill(80);
  double sum = 0;
  for (int i=0; i<vs.length; i++)
    sum += vs[i].capacity();
  System.out.println("Total capacity is " + sum);
  for (int i=0; i<vs.length; i++)
    System.out.println("vessel number " + i + ": " + vs[i]);
}
```

9.6   Field Declarations in Classes

The purpose of a *field* is to hold a value inside an object (if nonstatic) or a class (if static). A field must be declared in a class declaration. A *field-declaration* has one of the forms

> *field-modifiers   type   fieldname1, fieldname2, ... ;*
> *field-modifiers   type   fieldname1 = initializer1, ... ;*

The *field-modifiers* may be a list of the modifiers `static`, `final`, `transient` (section 21.11) and `volatile` and at most one of the access modifiers `private`, `protected`, and `public` (section 9.7).

If a field `f` in class `C` is declared `static`, then `f` is associated with the class `C` and can be referred to independently of any objects of class `C`. The field can be referred to as `C.f` or `o.f`, where `o` is an expression of type `C`, or, in the declaration of `C`, as `f`. If a field `f` in class `C` is not declared `static`, then `f` is associated with an *object* (also called *instance*) of class `C`, and every instance has its own instance of the field. The field can be referred to as `o.f`, where `o` is an expression of type `C`, or, in nonstatic code in the declaration of `C`, as `f`.

If a field `f` in class `C` is declared `final`, the field cannot be modified after initialization. If `f` has reference type and points to an object or array, the object's fields or the array's elements may still be modified. The initialization must happen either in the declaration or in an initializer block (section 9.10), or (if the field is nonstatic) precisely once in every constructor in class `C`.

A *field initializer* may be an expression or an array initializer (section 8.2). A static field initializer can refer only to static members of `C` and can throw no checked exceptions (chapter 14).

A field is given a *default initial value* depending on its type `t`. If `t` is a primitive type, the field is initialized to 0 (when `t` is `byte`, `char`, `short`, `int`, or `long`) or 0.0 (when `t` is `float` or `double`) or `false` (when `t` is `boolean`). If `t` is a reference type, the field is initialized to `null`.

Static fields are initialized when the class is loaded. First all static fields are given their default initial values, then the static initializer blocks (section 9.10) and static field initializers are executed, in order of appearance in the class declaration.

Nonstatic fields are initialized when a constructor is called, at which time all static fields have been initialized already (section 9.9).

If a class `C` declares a nonstatic field `f`, and `C` is a subclass of a class `B` that has a nonstatic field `f`, then every object of class `C` has two fields, both called `f`: one is the B-field `f` declared in the superclass `B`, and one is the C-field `f` declared in `C` itself. What field is referred to by a field access `o.f` is determined by the type of `o` (section 11.9).

9.7   The Member Access Modifiers `private`, `protected`, `public`

A member (field or method or nested class or interface) is always accessible in the class in which it is declared, except where shadowed by a variable or parameter or field (of a nested class). The *access modifiers* `private`, `protected`, and `public` determine where else the member is accessible.

If a member is declared `private` in top-level class `C` or a nested class within `C`, it is accessible in `C` and its nested classes, but not in their subclasses outside `C` nor in other classes. If a member in class `C` is declared `protected`, it is accessible in all classes in the same package (chapter 17) as `C` and in subclasses of `C`, but not in non-subclasses in other packages. If a member in class `C` is not declared `private`, `protected`, or `public`, it has *package access*, or *default access*, and is accessible only in classes within the same package as `C`, not in classes in other packages. If a member in class `C` is declared `public`, it is accessible in all classes, including classes in other packages. Thus, in order of increasing accessibility, we have `private` access, package (or default) access, `protected` access, and `public` access.

Example 21 Field Declarations
The SPoint class (example 17) declares a static field allpoints and two nonstatic fields x and y.

Example 30 declares a static field ps of array type double[]. Its field initializer allocates a six-element array and binds it to ps, and then the initializer block (section 9.10) stores some numbers into the array.

The Barrel class in example 80 declares two nonstatic fields radius and height. The fields are final and therefore must be initialized (which is done in the constructor).

Example 22 Several Fields with the Same Name
An object of class C here has two nonstatic fields called vf, one declared in the superclass B and one declared in C itself. Similarly, an object of class D has three nonstatic fields called vf. Class B and class C each have a static field called sf. Class D does not declare a static field sf, so in class D the name sf refers to the static field sf in the superclass C. Examples 35 and 45 use these classes.

```
class B                          // One nonstatic field vf, one static sf
{ int vf; static int sf; B(int i) { vf = i; sf = i+1; } }

class C extends B                // Two nonstatic fields vf, one static sf
{ int vf; static int sf; C(int i) { super(i+20); vf = i; sf = i+2; } }

class D extends C                // Three nonstatic fields vf
{ int vf; D(int i) { super(i+40); vf = i; sf = i+4; } }
```

Example 23 Member Access Modifiers
The vessel hierarchy in example 19 is unsatisfactory because everybody can read and modify the fields of a vessel object. Example 80 presents an improved version of the hierarchy in which (1) the contents field in Vessel is made private to prevent modification, (2) a new public method getContents permits reading the field, and (3) the fields of Tank and Barrel are declared protected to permit access from subclasses declared in other packages.

Since the field contents in Vessel is private, it is not accessible in the subclasses (Tank, Barrel, ...), but the subclasses still inherit the field. Thus every vessel subclass object has room for storing the field but can change and access it only by using the methods fill and getContents inherited from the abstract superclass.

Example 24 Private Member Accessibility
A private member is accessible everywhere inside the enclosing top-level class (and only there).

```
class Access {
  private static int x;
  static class SI {
    private static int y = x;      // Access private x from enclosing class
  }
  static void m() {
    int z = SI.y;                  // Access private y from nested class
  }
}
```

9.8   Method Declarations

A *method* must be declared inside a class. A *method-declaration* declaring method m has the form

> *method-modifiers return-type* m(*formal-list*) *throws-clause*
>   *method-body*

The *formal-list* is a comma-separated list of zero or more *formal parameter declarations*, of form

> *parameter-modifier type parameter-name*

The *parameter-modifier* may be final, meaning that the parameter cannot be modified inside the method, or absent. The *type* is any type. The *parameter-name* is any name, but the parameter names must be distinct. A formal parameter is an initialized variable; its scope is the *method-body*.

The method name m together with the list $t_1, \ldots, t_n$ of declared parameter types in the *formal-list* determine the *method signature* m($t_1, \ldots, t_n$). The *return-type* is not part of the method signature.

A class may declare more than one method with the same *method-name*, provided they have different method signatures. This is called *overloading* of the *method-name*.

The *method-body* is a *block-statement* (section 12.2) and thus may contain statements as well as declarations of variables and local classes. In particular, the *method-body* may contain return statements. If the *return-type* is void, the method does not return a value, and no return statement in the *method-body* can have an expression argument. If the *return-type* is not void but a type, the method must return a value: it must not be possible for execution to reach the end of *method-body* without executing a return statement. Moreover, every return statement must have an expression argument whose type is a subtype of the *return-type*.

The *method-modifiers* may be abstract or a list of static, final, synchronized (section 15.2), and at most one of the access modifiers private, protected, and public (section 9.7).

If a method m in class C is declared static, then m is associated with the class C; it can be referred to without any object. The method may be called as C.m(...) or as o.m(...), where o is an expression whose type is a subtype of C, or, inside methods, constructors, field initializers, and initializer blocks in C, simply as m(...). A static method can refer only to static fields and methods of the class.

If a method m in class C is not declared static, then m is associated with an object (instance) of class C. Outside the class, the method must be called as o.m(...), where o is an object of class C or a subclass, or, inside nonstatic methods, nonstatic field initializers, and nonstatic initializer blocks in C, simply as m(...). A nonstatic method can refer to all fields and methods of class C, whether they are static or not.

If a method m in class C is declared final, it cannot be overridden (redefined) in subclasses.

If a method m in class C is declared abstract, class C must itself be abstract (and so cannot be instantiated). An abstract method cannot be static, final, or synchronized, and its declaration has this form, without a method body:

> abstract *method-modifiers return-type* m(*formal-list*) *throws-clause*;

The *throws-clause* of a method or constructor has the form

> throws E1, E2, ...

where E1, E2, ... are the names of exception types covering all the checked exceptions that the method or constructor may throw. If execution may throw exception e, then e is either an unchecked exception (chapter 14) or a checked exception whose class is a subtype of one of E1, E2, ...

Example 25 Method Name Overloading and Signatures

This class declares four overloaded methods m whose signatures (section 5.5) are m(int) and m(boolean) and m(int, double) and m(double, double). Some of the overloaded methods are static, others nonstatic. The overloaded methods may have different return types, as shown here. Example 50 explains the method calls.

It would be legal to declare an additional method with signature m(double, int), but then the method call m(10, 20) would become ambiguous and illegal. Namely, there is no way to determine whether to call m(int, double) or m(double, int).

```
class Overloading {
  double m(int i) { return i; }
  boolean m(boolean b) { return !b; }
  static double m(int x, double y) { return x + y + 1; }
  static double m(double x, double y) { return x + y + 3; }

  public static void main(String[] args) {
    System.out.println(m(10, 20));          // Prints: 31.0
    System.out.println(m(10, 20.0));        // Prints: 31.0
    System.out.println(m(10.0, 20));        // Prints: 33.0
    System.out.println(m(10.0, 20.0));      // Prints: 33.0
  }
}
```

Example 26 Method Overriding

In the vessel hierarchy (example 19), the classes Tank and Barrel override the method toString inherited from the universal superclass Object, and class Cube overrides toString inherited from class Tank.

Example 27 Method Overriding and Overloading

The class C1 declares the overloaded method m1 with signatures m1(double) and m1(int), and the method m2 with signature m2(int). The subclass C2 hides C1's method m1(double) and overloads m2 by declaring an additional variant. Calls to these methods are shown in example 51.

```
class C1 {
  static void m1(double d) { System.out.println("11d"); }
  void m1(int i) { System.out.println("11i"); }
  void m2(int i) { System.out.println("12i"); }
}

class C2 extends C1 {
  static void m1(double d) { System.out.println("21d"); }
  void m1(int i) { System.out.println("21i"); }
  void m2(double d) { System.out.println("22d"); }
}
```

9.9 Constructor Declarations

The purpose of a constructor in class C is to initialize new objects (instances) of the class. A *constructor-declaration* in class C has the form

> *constructor-modifiers* C (*formal-list*) *throws-clause*
>   *constructor-body*

The *constructor-modifiers* may be a list of at most one of private, protected, and public (section 9.7); a constructor cannot be abstract, final, or static. A constructor has no return type.

Constructors may be overloaded in the same way as methods: the *constructor signature* (a list of the parameter types in *formal-list*) is used to distinguish constructors in the same class. A constructor may call another overloaded constructor in the same class using the syntax:

> this (*actual-list*)

but a constructor may not call itself, directly or indirectly. A call this (...) to another constructor, if present, must be the very first action of a constructor, preceding any declaration or statement.

The *constructor-body* is a *block-statement* (section 12.2) and so may contain statements as well as declarations of variables and local classes. The *constructor-body* may contain return statements, but no return statement can take an expression argument.

A class that does not explicitly declare a constructor implicitly declares a public, argumentless *default constructor* whose only (implicit) action is to call the superclass constructor (section 9.5):

> public C() { super(); }

The *throws-clause* of the constructor specifies the checked exceptions that may be thrown by the constructor, in the same manner as for methods (section 9.8).

When new creates a new object in memory (section 11.7), the object's nonstatic fields are given default initial values according to their type. Then a constructor is called to further initialize the object, and the following happens: First, some superclass constructor is called (explicitly or implicitly, see examples 29 and 52) exactly once, then the nonstatic field initializers and nonstatic initializer blocks are executed once in order of appearance in the class declaration, and finally the constructor body (except the explicit superclass constructor call, if any) is executed. The call to a superclass constructor will cause a call to a constructor in its superclass, and so on, until reaching Object().

9.10 Initializer Blocks, Field Initializers, and Initializers

In addition to field initializers (section 9.6), a class may contain *initializer-blocks*. Initializer blocks may be used when field initializers or constructors do not suffice. We use the term *initializer* to mean field initializers as well as initializer blocks. A *static initializer block* has the form

> static *block-statement*

The static initializer blocks and field initializers of static fields are executed, in order of appearance in the class declaration, when the class is loaded. A *nonstatic initializer block* is simply a free-standing *block-statement*. Nonstatic initializer blocks are executed after the constructor when an object is created (section 9.9).

An initializer is not allowed to throw a checked exception (chapter 14). If execution of a static initializer throws an (unchecked) exception during class loading, that exception is discarded and the exception ExceptionInInitializerError is thrown instead.

Example 28 Constructor Overloading; Calling Another Constructor
We add a new constructor to the Point class (example 16), thus overloading its constructors. The old constructor has signature Point(int, int) and the new one Point(Point). The new constructor makes a copy of the point p by calling the old constructor using the syntax this(p.x, p.y).

```
class Point {
  int x, y;

  Point(int x, int y)                  // Overloaded constructor
  { this.x = x; this.y = y; }

  Point(Point p)                       // Overloaded constructor
  { this(p.x, p.y); }                  // Calls the first constructor

  void move(int dx, int dy)
  { x += dx; y += dy; }

  public String toString()
  { return "(" + x + ", " + y + ")"; }
}
```

Example 29 Calling a Superclass Constructor
The constructor in the ColoredPoint subclass (example 71) calls its superclass constructor using the syntax super(x, y).

Example 30 Field Initializers and Initializer Blocks
Here the static field initializer allocates an array and binds it to field ps. The static initializer block fills the array with an increasing sequence of pseudo-random numbers, then scales them so that the last number is 1.0 (this is useful for generating rolls of a random loaded die). This cannot be done using the field initializer alone.

One could delete the two occurrences of static to obtain another example, with a nonstatic field ps, a nonstatic field initializer, and a nonstatic initializer block. However, it is more common for nonstatic fields to be initialized by a constructor.

```
class InitializerExample {
  static double[] ps = new double[6];

  static {                             // Static initializer block
    double sum = 0;
    for (int i=0; i<ps.length; i++)    // Fill with increasing random numbers
      ps[i] = sum += Math.random();
    for (int i=0; i<ps.length; i++)    // Scale so last ps element is 1.0
      ps[i] /= sum;
  }
  ...
}
```

9.11   Nested Classes, Member Classes, Local Classes, and Inner Classes

A nonstatic nested class, that is, a nonstatic member class NMC or a local class NLC in a nonstatic member, is called an *inner class*. An object of an inner class always contains a reference to an object of the enclosing class C, called the *enclosing object*. That object can be referred to as C.this (example 36), so a nonstatic member x of the enclosing object can be referred to as C.this.x.

An inner class or local class cannot have static members. More precisely, all static fields must also be final, and methods and nested classes in an inner class or local class must be nonstatic.

A static nested class, that is, a static member class SMC or a local class in a static member, has no enclosing object and cannot refer to nonstatic members of the enclosing class C. This is the standard restriction on static members of a class (section 9.1). A static member class may itself have static as well as nonstatic members.

If a local class refers to variables or formal parameters in the enclosing method or constructor or initializer, those variables or parameters must be final.

9.12   Anonymous Classes

An *anonymous class* is a special kind of local class; hence it must be declared inside a method or constructor or initializer. An anonymous class can be declared, and exactly one instance created, using the special expression syntax

```
new C (actual-list)
    class-body
```

where C is a class name. This creates an anonymous subclass of class C, with the given *class-body* (section 9.1). Moreover, it creates an object of that anonymous subclass and calls the appropriate C constructor with the arguments in *actual-list*, as if by super (*actual-list*). An anonymous class cannot declare its own constructors.

When I is an interface name, the similar expression syntax

```
new I ()
    class-body
```

creates an anonymous local class, with the given *class-body* (section 9.1), that must implement the interface I, and also creates an object of that anonymous class. Note that the parameter list after I must be empty.

Example 31 Member Classes and Local Classes

```
class TLC {                                 // Top-level class
  static int sf;
  int nf;
  static class SMC {                        // Static member class
    static int ssf = sf + TLC.sf;           // can have static members
    int snf = sf + TLC.sf;                  // cannot use nonstatic TLC members
  }
  class NMC {                               // Nonstatic member (inner) class
    int nnf1 = sf + nf;                     // can use nonstatic TLC members
    int nnf2 = TLC.sf + TLC.this.nf;        // cannot have static members
  }
  void nm() {                               // Nonstatic method in TLC
    class NLC {                             // Local (inner) class in method
      int m(int p) { return sf+nf+p; }      // can use nonstatic TLC members
} } }
```

Example 32 An Iterator as a Local Class
Method `suffixes` returns an object of the local class SuffixIterator, which implements the Iterator interface (section 20.7) to enumerate the nonempty suffixes of the string `s`:

```
class LocalInnerClassExample {
  public static void main(String[] args) {
    Iterator seq = suffixes(args[0]);
    while (seq.hasNext())
      System.out.println(seq.next());
  }
  static Iterator suffixes(final String s) {
    class SuffixIterator implements Iterator {
      int startindex=0;
      public boolean hasNext() { return startindex < s.length(); }
      public Object next() { return s.substring(startindex++); }
      public void remove() { throw new UnsupportedOperationException(); }
    }
    return new SuffixIterator();
} }
```

Example 33 An Iterator as an Anonymous Local Class
Alternatively, we may use an anonymous local class in method `suffixes`:

```
static Iterator suffixes(final String s) {
  return
    new Iterator() {
        int startindex=0;
        public boolean hasNext() { return startindex < s.length(); }
        public Object next() { return s.substring(startindex++); }
        public void remove() { throw new UnsupportedOperationException(); }
      };
}
```

10   Classes and Objects in the Computer

10.1   What Is a Class?

Conceptually, a class represents a concept, a template for creating instances (objects). In the computer, a class is a chunk of memory, set aside once, when the class is loaded at run-time. A class has the following parts:

- The name of the class.
- Room for all the static members of the class.

A class can be drawn as a box. The header `class SPoint` gives the class name, and the box itself contains the static members of the class:

10.2   What Is an Object?

Conceptually, an object is an instance of a concept (a class). In the computer, an object is a chunk of memory, set aside by an object creation expression `new C(...)`; see section 11.7. Every evaluation of an object creation expression `new C(...)` creates a distinct object, with its own chunk of computer memory. An object has the following parts:

- A reference to the *class* C of the object; this is the class C used when creating the object.
- Room for all the nonstatic members of the object.

An object can be drawn as a box. The header `: SPoint` gives the object's class (underlined), and the remainder of the box contains the nonstatic members of the object:

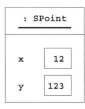

10.3   Inner Objects

When `NIC` is an inner class (a nonstatic member class, or a local class in nonstatic code) in a class C, then an object of class `NIC` is an *inner object*. In addition to the object's class and the nonstatic fields, an inner object will always contain a reference to an *enclosing object*, which is an object of the innermost enclosing class C. The enclosing object reference can be written `C.this` in Java programs.

An object of a static nested class, on the other hand, contains no reference to an enclosing object.

Example 34 Objects and Classes

This is the computer memory at the end of the `main` method in example 48, using the SPoint class from example 17. The variables `p` and `s` refer to the same object, variable `q` is null, and variable `r` refers to the rightmost object. No variable refers to the middle object; it will be removed by the garbage collector.

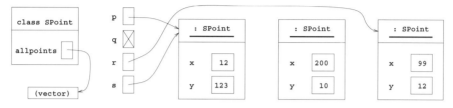

Example 35 Objects With Multiple Fields of the Same Name

This is the computer memory at the end of the `main` method in example 45, using the classes from example 22. The classes B and C each have a single static field `sf`; class D has none. The two objects of class C each have two nonstatic fields `vf` (called B/vf and C/vf below), and the class D object has three nonstatic fields `vf`.

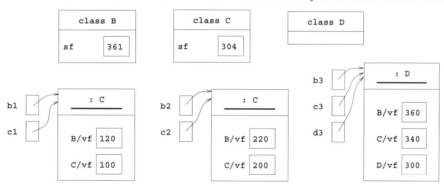

Example 36 Inner Objects

Example 31 declares a class TLC with nonstatic member (inner) class NMC and static member class SMC. If we create a TLC-object, two NMC-objects, and an SMC object,

```
TLC oo = new TLC();
TLC.NMC io1 = oo.new NMC(), io2 = oo.new NMC();
TLC.SMC sio = new TLC.SMC();
```

then the computer memory will contain these objects (the classes are not shown)

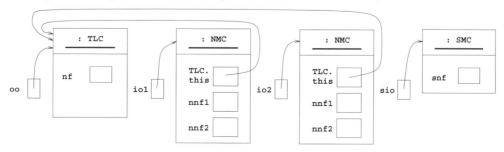

11 Expressions

An expression is evaluated to obtain a value (such as 117). In addition, evaluation of an expression may change the computer's *state*: the values of variables, fields, and array elements, the contents of files, and so on. More precisely, evaluation of an expression

- terminates normally, producing a value; or
- terminates abruptly by throwing an exception; or
- does not terminate at all (for instance, because it calls a method that does not terminate).

Expressions are built from *literals* (anonymous constants), variables, fields, operators, method calls, array accesses, conditional expressions, the new operator, and so on; see the table of expression forms on the facing page.

One must distinguish the compile-time *type of an expression* from the run-time *class of an object*. An expression has a type (chapter 5) inferred by the compiler. When this is a reference type t, and the value of the expression is an object o, then the class of object o will be a subtype of t but not necessarily equal to t. For instance, the expression (Number)(new Integer(2)) has type Number, but its value is an object whose class is Integer, a subclass of Number.

11.1 Table of Expression Forms

The table of expression forms shows the form, meaning, associativity, argument (operand) types, and result types for expressions. The expressions are grouped according to precedence, as indicated by the horizontal rules, from high precedence to low precedence. Higher-precedence forms are evaluated before lower-precedence forms. Parentheses may be used to emphasize or force a particular order of evaluation.

When an operator (such as +) is left-associative, a sequence e1 + e2 + e3 of operators is evaluated as if parenthesized (e1 + e2) + e3. When an operator (such as =) is right-associative, a sequence e1 = e2 = e3 of operators is evaluated as if parenthesized e1 = (e2 = e3).

In the argument type and result type columns of the table, *integer* stands for any of char, byte, short, int, or long; and *numeric* stands for integer or float or double.

For an operator with one integer or numeric operand, the *promotion type* is double if the operand has type double; it is float if the operand has type float; it is long if the operand has type long; otherwise it is int (that is, if the operand has type byte, char, short, or int).

For an operator with two integer or numeric operands (except the shift operators; section 11.4), the promotion type is double if any operand has type double; otherwise, it is float if any operand has type float; otherwise, it is long if any operand has type long; otherwise it is int.

Before the operation is performed, the operands are promoted, that is, converted to the promotion type by a widening type conversion (section 11.12.1).

If the result type is given as numeric also, it equals the promotion type. For example, 10 / 3 has type int, whereas 10 / 3.0 has type double, and c + (byte)1 has type int when c has type char.

Table of Expression Forms

Expression	Meaning	Associativity	Argument types	Result type
a[...]	array access (section 8.1)		t[], integer	t
o.f	field access (section 11.9)		object	type of f
o.m(...)	method call (section 11.11)		object	
x++	postincrement		numeric	numeric
x--	postdecrement		numeric	numeric
++x	preincrement		numeric	numeric
--x	predecrement		numeric	numeric
-x	negation (minus sign)	right	numeric	numeric
~e	bitwise complement	right	integer	int/long
!e	logical negation	right	boolean	boolean
new t[...]	array creation (section 8.1)		type	t[]
new C(...)	object creation (section 11.7)		class	C
(t)e	type cast (section 11.12)		type, any	t
e1 * e2	multiplication	left	numeric	numeric
e1 / e2	division	left	numeric	numeric
e1 % e2	remainder	left	numeric	numeric
e1 + e2	addition	left	numeric	numeric
e1 + e2	string concatenation	left	String, any	String
e1 + e2	string concatenation	left	any, String	String
e1 - e2	subtraction	left	numeric	numeric
e1 << e2	left shift (section 11.4)	left	integer	int/long
e1 >> e2	signed right shift	left	integer	int/long
e1 >>> e2	unsigned right shift	left	integer	int/long
e1 < e2	less than	none	numeric	boolean
e1 <= e2	less than or equal to	none	numeric	boolean
e1 >= e2	greater than or equal to	none	numeric	boolean
e1 > e2	greater than	none	numeric	boolean
e instanceof t	instance test (section 11.8)	none	any, reference type	boolean
e1 == e2	equal	left	compatible	boolean
e1 != e2	not equal	left	compatible	boolean
e1 & e2	bitwise and	left	integer	int/long
e1 & e2	logical strict and	left	boolean	boolean
e1 ^ e2	bitwise exclusive-or	left	integer	int/long
e1 ^ e2	logical strict exclusive-or	left	boolean	boolean
e1 | e2	bitwise or	left	integer	int/long
e1 | e2	logical strict or	left	boolean	boolean
e1 && e2	logical and (section 11.3)	left	boolean	boolean
e1 || e2	logical or (section 11.3)	left	boolean	boolean
e1 ? e2 : e3	conditional (section 11.6)	right	boolean, any, any	any
x = e	assignment (section 11.5)	right	e subtype of x	type of x
x += e	compound assignment	right	compatible	type of x

11.2   Arithmetic Operators

The value of the postincrement expression x++ is that of x, and its effect is to increment x by 1; and similarly for postdecrement x--. The value of the preincrement expression ++x is that of x+1, and its effect is to increment x by 1; and similarly for predecrement --x.

Integer division e1/e2 truncates, that is, rounds toward zero, so 10/3 is 3, and (-10)/3 is −3. The integer remainder x%y equals x-(x/y)*y when y is nonzero; it has the same sign as x. Integer division or remainder by zero throws the exception ArithmeticException. Integer overflow does not throw an exception but wraps around. Thus, in the int type, the expression 2147483647+1 evaluates to −2147483648, and the expression -2147483648-1 evaluates to 2147483647.

The floating-point remainder x%y roughly equals x-(((int)(x/y))*y when y is nonzero. Floating-point division by zero and floating-point overflow do not throw exceptions but produce special IEEE754 values (of type float or double) such as Infinity or NaN ("not a number").

11.3   Logical Operators

The operators == and != require the operand types to be compatible: one must be a subtype of the other. Two values of primitive type are equal (by ==) if they represent the same value after conversion to their common supertype. For instance, 10 and 10.0 are equal. Two values of reference type are equal (by ==) if both are null, or both are references to the same object or array, created by the same execution of the new-operator. Hence do not use == or != to compare strings: two strings s1 and s2 may contain the same sequence of characters and therefore be equal by s1.equals(s2), yet be distinct objects and therefore unequal by s1==s2 (example 5).

The logical operators && and || perform *shortcut evaluation*: if e1 evaluates to true in e1&&e2, then e2 is evaluated to obtain the value of the expression; otherwise e2 is ignored and the value of the expression is false. Conversely, if e1 evaluates to false in e1||e2, then e2 is evaluated to obtain the value of the expression; otherwise e2 is ignored and the value of the expression is true. By contrast, the operators & (logical strict and) and ^ (logical strict exclusive-or) and | (logical strict or) always evaluate both operands, regardless of the value of the left-hand operand. Usually the shortcut operators && and || are preferable.

11.4   Bitwise Operators and Shift Operators

The operators ~ (bitwise complement) and & (bitwise and) and ^ (bitwise exclusive-or) and | (bitwise or) may be used on operands of integer type. The operators work in parallel on all bits of the 2's complement representation of the operands. Thus ~n equals (-n)-1 and also equals (-1)^n.

The shift operators << and >> and >>> shift the bits of the 2's complement representation of the first argument. The two operands are promoted (section 11.1) separately, and the result type is the promotion type (int or long) of the first argument. Thus the shift operation is always performed on a 32-bit (int) or a 64-bit (long) value. In the former case, the length of the shift is between 0 and 31 as determined by the five least significant bits of the second argument; in the latter case, it is between 0 and 63 as determined by the six least significant bits of the second argument.

The left shift n<<s equals n*2*2*...*2 where there are s multiplications. The signed right shift n>>s of a non-negative n equals n/2/2/.../2 where there are s divisions; the signed right shift of a negative n equals ~((~n)>>s). The unsigned right shift n>>>s of a non-negative n equals n>>s; the signed right shift of a negative n equals (n>>s)+(2<<~s) if n has type int, and (n>>s)+(2L<<~s) if it has type long, where 2L is the long constant with value 2. See example 68 for clever and intricate use of bitwise operators — good style on a tiny embedded processor, but not in general.

Example 37 Arithmetic Operators

```
public static void main(String[] args) {
  int max = 2147483647;
  int min = -2147483648;
  println(max+1);                           // Prints: -2147483648
  println(min-1);                           // Prints:  2147483647
  println(-min);                            // Prints: -2147483648
  print(   10/3); println(   10/(-3));      // Prints:  3 -3
  print((-10)/3); println((-10)/(-3));      // Prints: -3  3
  print(   10%3); println(   10%(-3));      // Prints:  1  1
  print((-10)%3); println((-10)%(-3));      // Prints: -1 -1
}
static void print(int i)   { System.out.print(i + " "); }
static void println(int i) { System.out.println(i + " "); }
```

Example 38 Logical Operators

Because of shortcut evaluation of `&&`, this expression from example 12 does not evaluate the array access `days[mth-1]` unless $1 \le \text{mth} \le 12$, so the index is never out of bounds:

```
(mth >= 1) && (mth <= 12) && (day >= 1) && (day <= days[mth-1])
```

This method returns `true` if `y` is a leap year, namely, if `y` is a multiple of 4 but not of 100, or is a multiple of 400:

```
static boolean leapyear(int y)
{ return y % 4 == 0 && y % 100 != 0 || y % 400 == 0; }
```

Example 39 Bitwise Operators and Shift Operators

```
class Bitwise {
  public static void main(String[] args) throws Exception {
    int a = 0x3;                          // Bit pattern   0011
    int b = 0x5;                          // Bit pattern   0101
    println4(a);                          // Prints:       0011
    println4(b);                          // Prints:       0101
    println4(~a);                         // Prints:       1100
    println4(~b);                         // Prints:       1010
    println4(a & b);                      // Prints:       0001
    println4(a ^ b);                      // Prints:       0110
    println4(a | b);                      // Prints:       0111
  }
  static void println4(int n) {
    for (int i=3; i>=0; i--)
      System.out.print(n >> i & 1);
    System.out.println();
  }
}
```

11.5   Assignment Expressions

In the *assignment expression* x = e, the type of e must be a subtype of the type of x. The type of the expression is the same as the type of x. The assignment is executed by evaluating expression x and then e, and storing e's value in variable x, after a widening conversion (section 11.12) if necessary. When e is a compile-time constant of type byte, char, short, or int, and x has type byte, char, or short, a narrowing conversion is done automatically, provided the value of e is within the range representable in x (section 5.1). The value of the expression x = e is that of x after the assignment.

The assignment operator is right-associative, so the multiple assignment x = y = e has the same meaning as x = (y = e), that is, evaluate the expression e, assign its value to y, and then to x.

When e has reference type (object type or array type), only a reference to the object or array is stored in x. Thus the assignment x = e does not copy the object or array (example 41).

When x and e have the same type, the compound assignment x += e is equivalent to x = x + e; however, x is evaluated only once, so in a[i++] += e the variable i is incremented only once. When the type of x is t, different from the type of e, then x += e is equivalent to x = (t)(x + e), in which the intermediate result (x + e) is converted to type t (section 11.12); again x is evaluated only once. The other compound assignment operators -=, *=, and so on, are similar.

Since assignment associates to the right, and the value of sum += e is that of sum after the assignment, one can write ps[i] = sum += e to first increment sum by e and then store the result in ps[i] (example 30).

11.6   Conditional Expressions

The *conditional expression* e1 ? e2 : e3 is legal if e1 has type boolean, and e2 and e3 both have numeric types, or both have type boolean, or both have compatible reference types. The conditional expression is evaluated by first evaluating e1. If e1 evaluates to true, then e2 is evaluated (and not e3); otherwise e3 is evaluated. The resulting value is the value of the conditional expression.

11.7   Object Creation Expressions

The *object creation expression*

    new C(*actual-list*)

creates a new object of class C and then calls that constructor in class C whose signature matches the arguments in *actual-list*. The *actual-list* is evaluated from left to right to obtain a list of argument values. These argument values are bound to the constructor's parameters, an object of the class is created in the memory, the nonstatic fields are given default initial values according to their type, a superclass constructor is called explicitly or implicitly (examples 29 and 52), all nonstatic field initializers and initializer blocks are executed in order of appearance, and finally the constructor body is executed to initialize the object. The value of the constructor call expression is the newly created object, whose class is C.

When C is an inner class in class D, and o evaluates to an object of class D, then one may create a C-object inside o using the syntax o.new C(*actual-list*); see example 36.

11.8   Instance Test Expressions

The *instance test* e instanceof t is evaluated by evaluating e to a value v. If v is not null and is a reference to an object of class C, where C is a subtype of t, the result is true; otherwise false.

Example 40 Widening, Narrowing, and Truncation in Assignments

The assignment d = 12 performs a widening of 12 from int to double. The assignments b = 123 and b2 = 123+1 perform an implicit narrowing from int to byte, because the right-hand sides are compile-time constants. The assignment b2 = b1+1 would be illegal because b1+1 is not a compile-time constant. The assignment b2 = 123+5 would be illegal because, although 123+5 is a compile-time constant, its value is not representable as a byte (whose range is −128..127).

```
double d;
d = 12;                      // Widening conversion from int to double
byte b1 = 123;               // Narrowing conversion from int to byte
byte b2;
b2 = 123 + 1;                // Legal: 123+1 is a compile-time constant
b2 = (byte)(b1 + 1);         // Legal: (byte)(b1 + 1) has type byte
int x = 0;
x += 1.5;                    // Equivalent to: x = (int)(x + 1.5); thus adds 1 to x
```

Example 41 Assignment Does Not Copy Objects

This example uses the Point class from example 16. Assignment (and parameter passing) copies only the reference, not the object:

```
Point p1 = new Point(10, 20);
System.out.println("p1 is " + p1);     // Prints: p1 is (10, 20)
Point p2 = p1;                         // p1 and p2 refer to same object
p2.move(8, 8);
System.out.println("p2 is " + p2);     // Prints: p2 is (18, 28)
System.out.println("p1 is " + p1);     // Prints: p1 is (18, 28)
```

Example 42 Compound Assignment Operators

Compute the product of all elements of array xs:

```
static double multiply(double[] xs) {
  double prod = 1.0;
  for (int i=0; i<xs.length; i++)
    prod *= xs[i];                     // Equivalent to: prod = prod * xs[i]
  return prod;
}
```

Example 43 Conditional Expression

Return the absolute value of x (always non-negative):

```
static double absolute(double x)
{ return (x >= 0 ? x : -x); }
```

Example 44 Object Creation and Instance Test

```
Number n1 = new Integer(17);
Number n2 = new Double(3.14);
// The following statements print: false, true, false, true.
System.out.println("n1 is a Double:  " + (n1 instanceof Double));
System.out.println("n2 is a Double:  " + (n2 instanceof Double));
System.out.println("null is a Double: " + (null instanceof Double));
System.out.println("n2 is a Number:  " + (n2 instanceof Number));
```

11.9   Field Access Expressions

A *field access* must have one of these three forms:

```
f
C.f
o.f
```

where C is a class and o an expression of reference type.

A class may have several fields of the same name f (section 9.6, example 22, and example 45).

A field access f must refer to a static or nonstatic field declared in or inherited by a class whose declaration encloses the field access expression (when f has not been shadowed by a field in a nested enclosing class, or by a variable or parameter of the same name). The class declaring the field is the target class TC.

A field access C.f must refer to a static field in class C or a superclass of C. That class is the target class TC.

A field access o.f, where expression o has type C, must refer to a static or nonstatic field in class C or a superclass of C. That class is the target class TC. To evaluate the field access, the expression o is evaluated to obtain an object. If the field is static, the object is ignored and the value of o.f is the TC-field f. If the field is nonstatic, the value of o must be non-null and the value of o.f is found as the value of the TC-field f in object o.

It is informative to contrast a nonstatic field access and a nonstatic method call (section 11.11):

- In a nonstatic field access o.f, the field referred to is determined by the (compile-time) *type* of the object expression o.

- In a nonstatic call to a nonprivate method o.m(...), the method called is determined by the (run-time) *class* of the target object: the object to which o evaluates.

11.10   The Current Object Reference `this`

The name this may be used in nonstatic code to refer to the current object (section 9.1). When nonstatic code in a given object is executed, the object reference this refers to the object as a whole. Hence, when f is a field and m is a method (declared in the innermost enclosing class), then this.f means the same as f (when f has not been shadowed by a variable or parameter of the same name), and this.m(...) means the same as m(...).

When C is an inner class in an enclosing class D, then inside C the notation D.this refers to the D object enclosing the inner C object. See example 31 where TLC.this.nf refers to field nf of the enclosing class TLC.

Example 45 Field Access

Here we illustrate static and nonstatic field access in the classes B, C, and D from example 22. Note that the field referred to by an expression of form o.vf or o.sf is determined by the type of expression o, not the class of the object to which o evaluates.

```
public static void main(String[] args) {
  C c1 = new C(100);                    // c1 has type C; object has class C
  B b1 = c1;                            // b1 has type B; object has class C
  print(C.sf,  B.sf);                   // Prints: 102 121
  print(c1.sf, b1.sf);                  // Prints: 102 121
  print(c1.vf, b1.vf);                  // Prints: 100 120
  C c2 = new C(200);                    // c2 has type C; object has class C
  B b2 = c2;                            // b2 has type B; object has class C
  print(c2.sf, b2.sf);                  // Prints: 202 221
  print(c2.vf, b2.vf);                  // Prints: 200 220
  print(c1.sf, b1.sf);                  // Prints: 202 221
  print(c1.vf, b1.vf);                  // Prints: 100 120
  D d3 = new D(300);                    // d3 has type D; object has class D
  C c3 = d3;                            // c3 has type C; object has class D
  B b3 = d3;                            // b3 has type B; object has class D
  print(D.sf,  C.sf,  B.sf);            // Prints: 304 304 361
  print(d3.sf, c3.sf, b3.sf);           // Prints: 304 304 361
  print(d3.vf, c3.vf, b3.vf);           // Prints: 300 340 360
}
static void print(int x, int y) { System.out.println(x+" "+y); }
static void print(int x, int y, int z) { System.out.println(x+" "+y+" "+z); }
```

Example 46 Using this When Referring to Shadowed Fields

A common use of this is to refer to fields (this.x and this.y) that have been shadowed by parameters (x and y), especially in constructors; see the Point class (example 16):

```
class Point {
  int x, y;
  Point(int x, int y) { this.x = x; this.y = y; }
... }
```

Example 47 Using this to Pass the Current Object to a Method

In the SPoint class (example 17), the current object reference this is used in the constructor to add the newly created object to the array list allpoints, and it is used in the method getIndex to look up the current object in the array list:

```
class SPoint {
  static ArrayList allpoints = new ArrayList();
  int x, y;
  SPoint(int x, int y) { allpoints.add(this); this.x = x; this.y = y; }
  int getIndex() { return allpoints.indexOf(this); }
... }
```

11.11 Method Call Expressions

A *method call* expression, or *method invocation*, must have one of these five forms:

    m(*actual-list*)
    super.m(*actual-list*)
    C.m(*actual-list*)
    C.super.m(*actual-list*)
    o.m(*actual-list*)

where m is a method name, C is a class name, and o is an expression of reference type. The *actual-list* is a possibly empty comma-separated list of expressions, called the *arguments* or *actual parameters*. The *call signature* is $csig = m(t_1, \ldots, t_n)$, where $(t_1, \ldots, t_n)$ is the list of types of the n arguments in the *actual-list*.

Determining what method is actually called by a method call is complicated because (1) method names may be overloaded, each version of the method having a distinct signature; (2) methods may be overridden, that is, reimplemented in subclasses; (3) methods that are both nonstatic and nonprivate are called by dynamic dispatch, given a target object; and (4) a method call in a nested class may call a method declared in some enclosing class.

Section 11.11.1 describes argument evaluation and parameter passing, assuming the simple case where it is clear which method m is being called. Section 11.11.2 describes how to determine which method is being called in the general case.

11.11.1 Method Call: Parameter Passing

This section considers the evaluation of a method call m(*actual-list*) when it is clear which method m is called, and focuses on the parameter passing mechanism.

The call is evaluated by evaluating the expressions in the *actual-list* from left to right to obtain the argument values. These argument values are then bound to the corresponding parameters in the method's *formal-list*, in order of appearance. A widening conversion (section 11.12) occurs if the type of an argument expression is a subtype of the method's corresponding parameter type.

Java uses *call-by-value* to bind argument values to formal parameters, so the formal parameter holds a copy of the argument value. Thus if the method changes the value of a formal parameter, this change does not affect the argument. For an argument of reference type, the parameter holds a copy of the object reference or array reference, and hence the parameter refers to the same object or array as the actual argument expression. Thus if the method changes that object or array, the changes will be visible after the method returns (example 49).

A nonstatic method must be called with a target object, for example as o.m(*actual-list*), where the target object is the value of o, or as m(*actual-list*), where the target object is the current object reference this. In either case, during execution of the method body, this will be bound to the target object.

A static method is not called with a target object, and it is illegal to use the identifier this inside the body of a static method.

When the argument values have been bound to the formal parameters, the method body is executed. The value of the method call expression is the value returned by the method if its return type is non-void; otherwise the method call expression has no value. When the method returns, all parameters and local variables in the method are discarded.

Example 48 Calling Nonoverloaded, Nonoverridden Methods
This program uses the SPoint class from example 17. The static methods getSize and getPoint may be
called by prefixing them with the class name SPoint or an expression of type SPoint, such as q. They may be
called before any objects have been created. The nonstatic method getIndex must be called with an object, as
in r.getIndex(); then the method is executed with the current object reference this bound to r.

```
System.out.println("Number of points created: " + SPoint.getSize());
SPoint p = new SPoint(12, 123);
SPoint q = new SPoint(200, 10);
SPoint r = new SPoint(99, 12);
SPoint s = p;
q = null;
System.out.println("Number of points created: " + SPoint.getSize());
System.out.println("Number of points created: " + q.getSize());
System.out.println("r is point number " + r.getIndex());
for (int i=0; i<SPoint.getSize(); i++)
  System.out.println("SPoint number " + i + " is " + SPoint.getPoint(i));
```

Example 49 Parameter Passing Copies References, Not Objects and Arrays
In the method call m(p, d, a) shown here, the object reference held in p is copied to parameter pp of m, so p
and pp refer to the same object, the integer held in d is copied to dd, and the array reference held in a is copied
to aa. At the end of method m, the state of the computer memory is this:

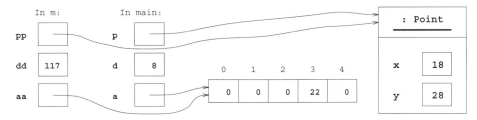

When method m returns, its parameters pp, dd, and aa are discarded. The variables p, d, and a are unmodified,
but the object and the array pointed to by p and a have been modified.

```
public static void main(String[] args) {
  Point p = new Point(10, 20);
  int[] a = new int[5];
  int d = 8;
  System.out.println("p is " + p);              // Prints: p is (10, 20)
  System.out.println("a[3] is " + a[3]);        // Prints: a[3] is 0
  m(p, d, a);
  System.out.println("p is " + p);              // Prints: p is (18, 28)
  System.out.println("d is " + d);              // Prints: d is 8
  System.out.println("a[3] is " + a[3]);        // Prints: a[3] is 22
}
static void m(Point pp, int dd, int[] aa) {
  pp.move(dd, dd);
  dd = 117;
  aa[3] = 22;
}
```

11.11.2   Method Call: Determining Which Method Is Called

In general, methods may be overloaded as well as overridden. The overloading is resolved at compile-time by finding the most specific applicable and accessible method signature for the call. Overriding (for nonstatic methods) is handled at run-time by searching the class hierarchy upwards starting with the class of the object on which the method is called.

At Compile-Time: Determine the Target Type and Signature

Find the target type TC. If the method call has the form m(*actual-list*), the target type TC is the innermost enclosing class containing a method called m that is visible (not shadowed by a method m, regardless of signature, in an intervening class). If the method call has the form super.m(*actual-list*), the target type TC is the superclass of the innermost enclosing class. If the method call has the form C.super.m(*actual-list*), the target type TC is the superclass of the enclosing class C. If the method call has the form C.m(*actual-list*), then TC is C. If the method call has the form o.m(*actual-list*), then TC is the type of the expression o.

 Find the target signature tsig. A method in class TC is *applicable* if its signature subsumes the call signature *csig* (section 5.5). Whether a method is *accessible* is determined by its access modifiers (section 9.7). Consider the collection of methods in TC that are both applicable and accessible. The call is illegal (method unknown) if there is no such method. The call is illegal (ambiguous) if there is more than one method whose extended signature $m(T, u_1, \ldots, u_n)$ is most specific, that is, one whose extended signature is subsumed by all the others. Thus if the call is legal, there is exactly one most specific extended signature; from that we obtain the target signature $tsig = m(u_1, \ldots, u_n)$.

 Determine whether the called method is static. If the method call has the form C.m(*actual-list*), the called method must be static. If the method call has the form m(*actual-list*) or o.m(*actual-list*) or super.m(*actual-list*) or C.super.m(*actual-list*), we use the target type TC and the signature *tsig* to determine whether the called method is static or nonstatic.

At Run-Time: Determine the Target Object (If Nonstatic) and Execute the Method

If the method is static, no target object is needed: the method to call is the method with signature *tsig* in class TC. However, when m is static in a method call o.m(*actual-list*), the expression o must be evaluated anyway, but its value is ignored.

 If the method is nonstatic, determine the target object; it will be bound to the object reference this during execution of the method. In the case of m(*actual-list*), the target object is this (if TC is the innermost class enclosing the method call), or TC.this (if TC is an outer class containing the method call). In the case of super.m(*actual-list*), the target object is this. In the case of C.super.m(*actual-list*), the target object is C.this. In the case o.m(*actual-list*), the expression o must evaluate to an object reference. If non-null, that object is the target object; otherwise the exception NullPointerException is thrown. If the method is nonprivate, the class hierarchy is searched to determine which method to call, starting with the class RTC of the target object. If a method with signature *tsig* is not found in class RTC, then the immediate superclass of RTC is searched, and so on. This search procedure is called *dynamic dispatch*. If the method is private, it must be in the target class TC and no search is needed.

 When the method has been determined, arguments are evaluated and bound as described in section 11.11.1.

Example 50 Calling Overloaded Methods
Here we call the overloaded methods m declared in example 25. The call m(10, 20) has call signature m(int, int) and thus calls the method with signature m(int, double), which is the most specific applicable one. Hence the first two lines call the method with signature m(int, double), and the last two call the method with signature m(double, double).

```
System.out.println(m(10, 20));          // Prints: 31.0
System.out.println(m(10, 20.0));        // Prints: 31.0
System.out.println(m(10.0, 20));        // Prints: 33.0
System.out.println(m(10.0, 20.0));      // Prints: 33.0
```

Example 51 Calling Overridden and Overloaded Methods
Here we use the classes C1 and C2 from example 27. The target type of c1.m1(i) is class C1, which has a nonstatic method with signature m1(int), so the call is to a nonstatic method; the target object has class C2, so the called method is m1(int) in C2; and quite similarly for c2.m1(i). The target type for c1.m1(d) is the class C1, which has a static method with signature m1(double), so the call is to a static method, and the object bound to c1 does not matter. Similarly for c2.m1(d), whose target type is C2, so it calls m1(double) in C2, which overrides m1(double) in C1.

The call c1.m2(i) has target type C1 and calls m2(int). However, a call c2.m2(i), whose target class is C2, would be ambiguous and illegal: the applicable extended signatures are m2(C1,int) and m2(C2,double), none of which is more specific than the other.

```
int i = 17;
double d = 17.0;
C2 c2 = new C2();                       // Type C2, object class C2
C1 c1 = c2;                             // Type C1, object class C1
c1.m1(i); c2.m1(i); c1.m1(d); c2.m1(d); // Prints: 21i 21i 11d 21d
c1.m2(i);                               // Prints: 12i
```

Example 52 Calling Overridden Methods from a Constructor
If d2 is an object of class D2, then calling d2.m2() will call the method m2 inherited from superclass D1. The call m1() in m2 is equivalent to this.m1(), where this equals d2, so the method m1 declared in class D2 is called. Hence the call d2.m2() will print D1.m2 and then D2.m1:7. It prints 7 because field f is initialized to 7 in constructor D2().

Perhaps more surprisingly, the creation d2 = new D2() of an object of class D2 will print D1.m2 and then D2.m1:0. Why does it print 0, not 7? The very first action of constructor D2() is to make an implicit call to the superclass constructor D1(), even *before* executing the assignment f = 7. Hence f will still have its default value 0 when method m1 in D2 is called from method m2 in D1, which in turn is called from constructor D1().

```
class D1 {
  D1() { m2(); }
  void m1() { System.out.println("D1.m1 "); }
  void m2() { System.out.print("D1.m2 "); m1(); }
}

class D2 extends D1 {
  int f;
  D2() { f = 7; }
  void m1() { System.out.println("D2.m1:" + f); }
}
```

11.12   Type Cast Expressions and Type Conversion

A *type conversion* converts a value from one type to another. A *widening* conversion converts from a type to a supertype. A *narrowing* conversion converts from a type to another type. This requires an explicit *type cast* (except in an assignment x = e or initialization where e is a compile-time integer constant; see section 11.5).

11.12.1   Type Cast Between Primitive Types

When e is an expression of primitive type and t is a primitive type, then a *type cast* of e to t is done using the expression

    (t)e

This expression, when legal, has type t. The legal type casts between primitive types are shown in the following table, where C marks a narrowing conversion that requires a type cast (t)e, W marks a widening conversion that preserves the value, and L marks a widening conversion that may cause a loss of precision.

From Type	To Type						
	char	byte	short	int	long	float	double
char	W	C	C	W	W	W	W
byte	C	W	W	W	W	W	W
short	C	C	W	W	W	W	W
int	C	C	C	W	W	L	W
long	C	C	C	C	W	L	L
float	C	C	C	C	C	W	W
double	C	C	C	C	C	C	W

A narrowing integer conversion discards those (most significant) bits that cannot be represented in the smaller integer type. Conversion from an integer type to a floating-point type (float or double) produces a floating-point approximation of the integer value. Conversion from a floating-point type to an integer type discards the fractional part of the number; that is, it rounds toward zero. When converting a too-large floating-point number to a long or int, the result is the best approximation (that is, the type's largest positive or the largest negative representable number); conversion to byte or short or char is done by converting to int and then to the requested type. The primitive type boolean cannot be cast to any other type. A type cast between primitive types never fails at run-time.

11.12.2   Type Cast Between Reference Types

When e is an expression of reference type and t is a reference type (class or interface or array type), a *type cast* of e to t is done using the expression

    (t)e

This expression has type t. It is evaluated by evaluating e to a value v. If v is null or is a reference to an object or array whose class is a subtype of t, then the type cast succeeds with result v; otherwise the exception ClassCastException is thrown. The type cast is illegal when it cannot possibly succeed at run-time, for instance, when e has type Double and t is Boolean: none of these classes is a subtype of the other.

12 Statements

A *statement* may change the computer's *state*: the value of variables, fields, array elements, the contents of files, and so on. More precisely, execution of a statement

- terminates normally (meaning execution will continue with the next statement, if any); or
- terminates abruptly by throwing an exception; or
- exits by executing a `return` statement (if inside a method or constructor); or
- exits a switch or loop by executing a `break` statement (if inside a switch or loop); or
- exits the current iteration of a loop and starts a new iteration by executing a `continue` statement (if inside a loop); or
- does not terminate at all, for instance, by executing `while (true) {}`.

12.1 Expression Statements

An *expression statement* is an *expression* followed by a semicolon:

>   *expression* ;

It is executed by evaluating the *expression* and ignoring its value. The only forms of *expression* that may be legally used in this way are assignment expressions (section 11.5), increment and decrement expressions (section 11.2), method call expressions (section 11.11), and object creation expressions (section 11.7).

For example, an assignment statement `x=e;` is an assignment expression `x=e` followed by a semicolon.

Similarly, a method call statement is a method call expression followed by semicolon. The value returned by the method, if any, is discarded; the method is executed only for its side effect.

12.2 Block Statements

A *block-statement* is a sequence of zero or more *statements* or *variable-declarations* or *class-declarations*, in any order, enclosed in braces:

>   {
>   *statements*
>   *class-declarations*
>   *variable-declarations*
>   }

12.3 The Empty Statement

An *empty statement* consists of a semicolon only. It is equivalent to the block statement { } that contains no statements or declarations, and it has no effect at all:

>   ;

12.4   Choice Statements

12.4.1   The `if` Statement

An if statement has the form

> if (*condition*)
>   *truebranch*

The *condition* must have type `boolean`, and *truebranch* is a statement. If *condition* evaluates to `true`, then *truebranch* is executed, otherwise not.

12.4.2   The `if-else` Statement

An if-else statement has the form:

> if (*condition*)
>   *truebranch*
> else
>   *falsebranch*

The *condition* must have type `boolean`, and *truebranch* and *falsebranch* are statements. If *condition* evaluates to `true`, then *truebranch* is executed; otherwise *falsebranch* is executed.

12.4.3   The `switch` Statement

A switch statement has the form

```
switch (expression) {
case constant1:  branch1
case constant2:  branch2
...
default:  branchn
}
```

The *expression* must have type `int`, `short`, `char`, or `byte`. Each *constant* must be a *compile-time constant* expression, consisting only of literals, final variables, final fields declared with explicit field initializers, and operators. No two *constants* may have the same value. The type of each *constant* must be a subtype of the type of *expression*.

Each *branch* is preceded by one or more case clauses and is a possibly empty sequence of statements, usually terminated by break or return (if inside a method or constructor) or continue (inside a loop). The default clause may be left out.

The switch statement is executed as follows: The *expression* is evaluated to obtain a value v. If v equals one of the *constants*, then the corresponding *branch* is executed. If v does not equal any of the *constants*, then the *branch* following default is executed; if there is no default clause, nothing is executed. If a *branch* is not exited by break or return or continue, then execution continues with the next *branch* in the switch regardless of the case clauses, until a *branch* exits or the switch ends.

Example 53 Block Statements

All method bodies and constructor bodies are block statements. In method sum from example 2, the *truebranch* of the second if statement is a block statement. Method m4 in example 4 contains two block statements, each of which contains a (local) declaration of variable x.

Example 54 Single if-else Statement

This method behaves the same as absolute in example 43:

```
static double absolute(double x) {
  if (x >= 0)
    return x;
  else
    return -x;
}
```

Example 55 Sequence of if-else Statements

We cannot use a switch here, because a switch can work only on integer types (including char):

```
static int wdayno1(String wday) {
  if      (wday.equals("Monday"))    return 1;
  else if (wday.equals("Tuesday"))   return 2;
  else if (wday.equals("Wednesday")) return 3;
  else if (wday.equals("Thursday"))  return 4;
  else if (wday.equals("Friday"))    return 5;
  else if (wday.equals("Saturday"))  return 6;
  else if (wday.equals("Sunday"))    return 7;
  else return -1;                            // Here used to mean 'not found'
}
```

Example 56 A switch Statement

Here we could have used a sequence of if-else statements, but a switch is both faster and clearer:

```
static String findCountry(int prefix) {
  switch (prefix) {
  case 1:   return "North America";
  case 44:  return "Great Britain";
  case 45:  return "Denmark";
  case 299: return "Greenland";
  case 46:  return "Sweden";
  case 7:   return "Russia";
  case 972: return "Israel";
  default:  return "Unknown";
  }
}
```

12.5   Loop Statements

12.5.1   The `for` Statement

A `for` statement has the form

>   for (*initialization*; *condition*; *step*)
>   *body*

where *initialization* is a *variable-declaration* (section 6.2) or an *expression*, *condition* is an *expression* of type `boolean`, *step* is an *expression*, and *body* is a *statement*. More generally, the *initialization* and *step* may also be comma-separated lists of *expressions*; the expressions in such a list are evaluated from left to right when the list is evaluated. The *initialization*, *condition*, and *step* may be empty. An empty *condition* is equivalent to `true`. Thus `for (;;)` *body* means "forever execute *body*." The `for` statement is executed as follows:

1. The *initialization* is executed.
2. The *condition* is evaluated. If it is `false`, the loop terminates.
3. If it is `true`, then
   a. The *body* is executed.
   b. The *step* is executed.
   c. Execution continues at (2).

12.5.2   The `while` Statement

A `while` statement has the form

>   while (*condition*)
>   *body*

where *condition* is an expression of type `boolean`, and *body* is a statement. It is executed as follows:

1. The *condition* is evaluated. If it is `false`, the loop terminates.
2. If it is `true`, then
   a. The *body* is executed.
   b. Execution continues at (1).

12.5.3   The `do-while` Statement

A `do-while` statement has the form

>   do
>   *body*
>   while (*condition*);

where *condition* is an expression of type `boolean`, and *body* is a statement. The *body* is executed at least once, because the `do-while` statement is executed as follows:

1. The *body* is executed.
2. The *condition* is evaluated. If it is `false`, the loop terminates.
3. If it is `true`, then execution continues at (1).

Example 57 Nested `for` Loops
This program prints a four-line triangle of asterisks (`*`):

```
for (int i=1; i<=4; i++) {
  for (int j=1; j<=i; j++)
    System.out.print ("*");
  System.out.println ();
}
```

Example 58 Array Search Using a `while` Loop
This method behaves the same as `wdayno1` in example 55:

```
static int wdayno2 (String wday) {
  int i=0;
  while (i < wdays.length && ! wday.equals(wdays[i]))
    i++;
  // Now i >= wdays.length or wday equal to wdays[i]
  if (i < wdays.length)
    return i+1;
  else
    return -1;                          // Here used to mean 'not found'
}

static final String[] wdays =
{ "Monday", "Tuesday", "Wednesday", "Thursday", "Friday", "Saturday", "Sunday" };
```

Example 59 Infinite Loop Because of Misplaced Semicolon
Here a misplaced semicolon (`;`) creates an empty loop body statement, where the increment `i++` is not part of the loop. Hence it will not terminate but will loop forever.

```
int i=0;
while (i<10);
  i++;
```

Example 60 Using `do-while`
Roll a die and compute `sum` until 5 or 6 comes up. Here we can use `do-while` but `while` is usually safer because it tests the loop condition before executing the loop body.

```
static int waitsum() {
  int sum = 0, eyes;
  do {
    eyes = (int)(1 + 6 * Math.random());
    sum += eyes;
  } while (eyes < 5);
  return sum;
}
```

12.6   Returns, Labeled Statements, Exits, and Exceptions

12.6.1   The `return` Statement

The simplest form of a return statement, without an expression argument, is

```
return;
```

That form of `return` statement must occur inside the body of a method whose return type is `void`, or inside the body of a constructor. Execution of the `return` statement exits the method or constructor and continues execution at the place from which the method or constructor was called.

Alternatively, a `return` statement may have an expression argument:

```
return expression;
```

That form of `return` statement must occur inside the body of a method (not constructor) whose return type is a supertype of the type of the *expression*. The `return` statement is executed as follows: First the *expression* is evaluated to some value v. Then it exits the method and continues execution at the method call expression that called the method; the value of that expression will be v.

12.6.2   Labeled Statements

A labeled statement has the form

```
label : statement
```

where *label* is a name. The scope of *label* is *statement*, where it can be used in `break` (section 12.6.3) and `continue` (section 12.6.4). The *label* cannot be reused inside *statement*, except inside a local class.

12.6.3   The `break` Statement

A break statement is legal only inside a switch or loop and has one of the forms

```
break;
break label;
```

Executing `break` exits the innermost enclosing switch or loop and continues execution after that switch or loop. Executing `break` *label* exits the enclosing statement that has label *label*, and continues execution after that statement. Such a statement must exist in the innermost enclosing method, constructor, or initializer block.

12.6.4   The `continue` Statement

A continue statement is legal only inside a loop and has one of the forms

```
continue;
continue label;
```

Executing `continue` terminates the current iteration of the innermost enclosing loop and continues the execution at the *step* in for loops (section 12.5.1) or the *condition* in while and do-while loops (sections 12.5.2 and 12.5.3). Executing `continue` *label* terminates the current iteration of the enclosing loop that has label *label*, and continues the execution at the *step* or the *condition*. There must be such a loop in the innermost enclosing method or constructor or initializer block.

Example 61 Using `return` to Terminate a Loop Early
This method behaves the same as `wdayno2` in example 58:

```
static int wdayno3(String wday) {
  for (int i=0; i < wdays.length; i++)
    if (wday.equals(wdays[i]))
      return i+1;
  return -1;                                // Here used to mean 'not found'
}
```

Example 62 Using `break` to Terminate a Loop Early

```
double prod = 1.0;
for (int i=0; i<xs.length; i++) {
  prod *= xs[i];
  if (prod == 0.0)
    break;
}
```

Example 63 Using `continue` to Start a New Iteration
This method decides whether `query` is a substring of `target`. When a mismatch between the strings is found, `continue` starts the next iteration of the outer `for` loop, thus incrementing `j`:

```
static boolean substring1(String query, String target) {
  nextposition:
    for (int j=0; j<=target.length()-query.length(); j++) {
      for (int k=0; k<query.length(); k++)
        if (target.charAt(j+k) != query.charAt(k))
          continue nextposition;
      return true;
    }
  return false;
}
```

Example 64 Using `break` to Exit a Labeled Statement Block
This method behaves as `substring1` from example 63. It uses `break` to exit the entire statement block labeled `thisposition`, thus skipping the first `return` statement and starting a new iteration of the outer `for` loop:

```
static boolean substring2(String query, String target) {
  for (int j=0; j<=target.length()-query.length(); j++)
    thisposition: {
      for (int k=0; k<query.length(); k++)
        if (target.charAt(j+k) != query.charAt(k))
          break thisposition;
      return true;
    }
  return false;
}
```

12.6.5   The **throw** Statement

A throw statement has the form

    throw *expression*;

where the type of the *expression* must be a subtype of class Throwable (chapter 14). The throw statement is executed as follows: The *expression* is evaluated to obtain an exception object v. If it is null, then a NullPointerException is thrown; otherwise the exception object v is thrown. Thus a thrown exception is never null. In any case, the enclosing block statement terminates abruptly (chapter 14). The thrown exception may be caught in a dynamically enclosing try-catch statement (section 12.6.6). If the exception is not caught, then the entire program execution will be aborted, and information from the exception will be printed on the console (for example, at the command prompt, or in the Java Console inside a Web browser).

12.6.6   The **try-catch-finally** Statement

A try-catch statement is used to catch (particular) exceptions thrown by the execution of a block of code. It has the following form:

    try
        body
    catch (E1 x1) *catchbody*₁
    catch (E2 x2) *catchbody*₂
    ...
    finally *finallybody*

where E1, E2, ... are names of exception types, x1, x2, ... are variable names, and *body*, *catchbody*$_i$, and *finallybody* are *block-statements* (section 12.2). There can be zero or more catch clauses, and the finally clause may be absent, but at least one catch or finally clause must be present.

We say that Ei matches exception type E if E is a subtype of Ei (possibly equal to Ei).

The try-catch-finally statement is executed by executing the *body*. If the execution of the *body* terminates normally, or exits by return or break or continue (when inside a method or constructor or switch or loop), then the catch clauses are ignored. If the *body* terminates abruptly by throwing exception e of class E, then the first matching Ei (if any) is located, variable xi is bound to e, and the corresponding *catchbody*$_i$ is executed. The *catchbody*$_i$ may terminate normally, or loop, or exit by executing return or break or continue, or throw an exception (possibly xi); if there is no finally clause, this determines how the entire try-catch statement terminates. A thrown exception e is never null (section 12.6.5), so xi is guaranteed not to be null either. If there is no matching Ei, then the entire try-catch statement terminates abruptly with exception e.

If there is a finally clause, then *finallybody* will be executed regardless of whether the execution of *body* terminated normally, regardless of whether *body* exited by executing return or break or continue (when inside a method or constructor or switch or loop), regardless of whether any exception thrown by *body* was caught by a catch clause, and regardless of whether the catch clause exited by executing return or break or continue or by throwing an exception. If execution of *finallybody* terminates normally, then the entire try-catch-finally terminates as determined by *body* (or *catchbody*$_i$, if one was executed and terminated abruptly or exited). If execution of *finallybody* terminates abruptly, then that determines how the entire try-catch-finally terminates (example 74).

Example 65 Throwing an Exception to Indicate Failure

Instead of returning the bogus error value -1 as in method wdayno3 (example 61), throw a WeekdayException (example 73). Note the throws clause (section 9.8) in the method header.

```
static int wdayno4(String wday) throws WeekdayException {
  for (int i=0; i < wdays.length; i++)
    if (wday.equals(wdays[i]))
      return i+1;
  throw new WeekdayException(wday);
}
```

Example 66 A try-catch Statement

This example calls the method wdayno4 (example 65) inside a try-catch statement that catches exceptions of class WeekdayException (example 73) and its superclass Exception. The second catch clause will be executed (for example) if the array access args[0] fails because there is no command line argument (since ArrayIndexOutOfBoundsException is a subclass of Exception). If an exception is caught, it is bound to the variable x and printed by an implicit call (chapter 7) to the exception's toString-method.

```
public static void main(String[] args) {
  try {
    System.out.println(args[0] + " is weekday number " + wdayno4(args[0]));
  } catch (WeekdayException x) {
    System.out.println("Weekday problem: " + x);
  } catch (Exception x) {
    System.out.println("Other problem: " + x);
  }
}
```

Example 67 A try-finally Statement

This method attempts to read three lines from a text file (section 21.4), each containing a single floating-point number. Regardless of whether anything goes wrong during reading (premature end-of-file, ill-formed number), the finally clause will close the readers before the method returns. It would do so even if the return statement were inside the try block.

```
static double[] readRecord(String filename) throws IOException {
  Reader freader        = new FileReader(filename);
  BufferedReader breader = new BufferedReader(freader);
  double[] res = new double[3];
  try {
    res[0] = new Double(breader.readLine()).doubleValue();
    res[1] = new Double(breader.readLine()).doubleValue();
    res[2] = new Double(breader.readLine()).doubleValue();
  } finally {
    breader.close();
  }
  return res;
}
```

12.7   The `assert` Statement

The `assert` statement has one of the following forms:

```
assert boolean-expression ;
assert boolean-expression : expression ;
```

The *boolean-expression* must have type `boolean`. The *expression* must have type `boolean`, `char`, `double`, `float`, `int`, `long`, or `Object`.

Under ordinary execution of a program, an `assert` statement has no effect at all. However, assertions may be enabled at run-time by specifying the option `-ea` or `-enableassertions` when executing a program `C` (chapter 16):

```
java -enableassertions C
```

When assertions are enabled at run-time, every execution of the `assert` statement will evaluate the *boolean-expression*. If the result is `true`, program execution continues normally. If the result is `false`, the assertion fails and an AssertionError will be thrown; moreover, in the second form of the `assert` statement, the *expression* will be evaluated and its value will be passed to the appropriate AssertionError constructor. Thus the value of the *expression* will be reported along with the exception in case of assertion failure. This simplifies troubleshooting in a malfunctioning program.

An AssertionError signals the failure of a fundamental assumption in the program and should not be caught by a `try-catch` statement in the program; it should be allowed to propagate to the toplevel.

An `assert` statement can serve two purposes: to document the programmer's assumption about the state at a certain point in the program, and to check (at run-time) that that assumption holds (provided the program is executed using the `enableassertions` option).

One may put an `assert` statement after a particularly complicated piece of code, to check that it has achieved what it was supposed to (example 68).

In a class that has a data representation invariant, one may assert the invariant at the end of every method in the class (example 69).

One should not use `assert` statements to check the validity of user input or the arguments of public methods or constructors, because the check would be performed only if assertions are enabled at run-time. Instead, use ordinary `if` statements and throw an exception in case of error.

The `assert` statement was introduced in Java 2, version 1.4, and cannot be used in Java compilers prior to that. A program using the `assert` statement must be compiled (section 16) with option `-source 1.4`, as follows:

```
javac -source 1.4 myprog.java
```

Example 68 Using `assert` to Specify and Check the Result of an Algorithm

The integer square root of $x \geq 0$ is an integer y such that $y^2 \leq x$ and $(y+1)^2 > x$. The precondition $x \geq 0$ is always checked, using an `if` statement. The postcondition on y is specified by an `assert` statement, and checked if assertions are enabled at run-time — which is reassuring, given that the correctness is none too obvious. The assertion uses casts to `long` to avoid arithmetic overflow.

```
static int sqrt(int x) {   // Algorithm by Borgerding, Hsieh, Ulery
  if (x < 0)
    throw new IllegalArgumentException("sqrt: negative argument");
  int temp, y = 0, b = 0x8000, bshft = 15, v = x;;
  do {
    if (v >= (temp = (y<<1)+b << bshft--)) {
      y += b; v -= temp;
    }
  } while ((b >>= 1) > 0);
  assert (long)y * y <= x && (long)(y+1)*(y+1) > x;
  return y;
}
```

Example 69 Using `assert` to Specify and Check Invariants

A word list is a sequence of words to be formatted as a line of text. Its `length` is the minimum number of characters needed to format the words and the interword spaces, that is, the lengths of the words plus the number of words minus 1. Those methods that change the word list use `assert` statements to specify the invariant on `length` and check it if assertions are enabled at run-time.

```
class WordList {
  private LinkedList strings = new LinkedList();
  private int length = -1;              // Invariant: equals word lengths plus interword spaces

  public int length() { return length; }

  public void addLast(String s) {
    strings.addLast(s);
    length += 1 + s.length();
    assert length == computeLength() + strings.size() - 1;
  }

  public String removeFirst() {
    String res = (String)strings.removeFirst();
    length -= 1 + res.length();
    assert length == computeLength() + strings.size() - 1;
    return res;
  }
  private int computeLength() { ... } // For checking the invariant only
}
```

An algorithm for formatting a sequence of words into a text with a straight right-hand margin should produce lines res of a specified length `lineWidth`, unless there is only one word on the line or the line is the last one. This requirement can be expressed and checked using an `assert` statement (see the example file for details of the formatting algorithm itself):

```
assert res.length()==lineWidth || wordCount==1 || !wordIter.hasNext();
```

13 Interfaces

13.1 Interface Declarations

An *interface* describes fields and methods but does not implement them. An *interface-declaration* may contain field descriptions, method descriptions, class declarations, and interface declarations, in any order.

```
interface-modifiers interface I extends-clause {
    field-descriptions
    method-descriptions
    class-declarations
    interface-declarations
}
```

An interface may be declared at toplevel or inside a class or interface but not inside a method or constructor or initializer. At toplevel, the *interface-modifiers* may be public or absent. A public interface is accessible also outside its package. Inside a class or interface, the *interface-modifiers* may be static (always implicitly understood) and at most one of public, protected, or private.

The *extends-clause* may be absent or have the form

```
extends I1, I2, ...
```

where I1, I2, ... is a nonempty list of interface names. If the *extends-clause* is present, then interface I describes all those members described by I1, I2, ..., and interface I is a *subinterface* (and hence subtype) of I1, I2, ... Interface I can describe additional fields and methods but cannot override inherited members.

A *field-description* in an interface declares a named constant and must have the form

```
field-desc-modifiers type f = initializer;
```

where *field-desc-modifiers* is a list of static, final, and public, none of which needs to be given explicitly, as all are implicitly understood. The field initializer must be an expression involving only literals and operators, and static members of classes and interfaces.

A *method-description* for method m must have the form

```
method-desc-modifiers return-type m(formal-list) throws-clause;
```

where *method-desc-modifiers* is a list of abstract and public, both of which are understood and need not be given explicitly.

A *class-declaration* inside an interface is always implicitly static and public.

13.2 Classes Implementing Interfaces

A class C may be declared to implement one or more interfaces by an *implements-clause*:

```
class C implements I1, I2, ...
    class-body
```

In this case, C is a subtype (section 5.4) of I1, I2, and so on, and C must declare all the methods described by I1, I2, ... with exactly the prescribed signatures and return types. A class may implement any number of interfaces. Fields, classes, and interfaces declared in I1, I2, ... can be used in class C.

Example 70 Three Interface Declarations
The Colored interface describes method getColor, interface Drawable describes method draw, and Colored-Drawable describes both. The methods are implicitly public.

```
import java.awt.*;
interface Colored { Color getColor(); }
interface Drawable { void draw(Graphics g); }
interface ColoredDrawable extends Colored, Drawable {}
```

Example 71 Classes Implementing Interfaces
The methods getColor and draw must be public as in the interface declarations (example 70).

```
class ColoredPoint extends Point implements Colored {
  Color c;
  ColoredPoint(int x, int y, Color c) { super(x, y); this.c = c; }
  public Color getColor() { return c; }
}

class ColoredDrawablePoint extends ColoredPoint implements ColoredDrawable {
  Color c;
  ColoredDrawablePoint(int x, int y, Color c) { super(x, y, c); }
  public void draw(Graphics g) { g.fillRect(x, y, 1, 1); }
}

class ColoredRectangle implements ColoredDrawable {
  int x1, x2, y1, y2;    // (x1, y1) upper left, (x2, y2) lower right corner
  Color c;

  ColoredRectangle(int x1, int y1, int x2, int y2, Color c)
  { this.x1 = x1; this.y1 = y1; this.x2 = x2; this.y2 = y2; this.c = c; }
  public Color getColor() { return c; }
  public void draw(Graphics g) { g.drawRect(x1, y1, x2-x1, y2-y1); }
}
```

Example 72 Using Interfaces as Types
A Colored value has a getColor method; a ColoredDrawable value has a getColor method and a draw method:

```
static void printcolors(Colored[] cs) {
  for (int i=0; i<cs.length; i++)
    System.out.println(cs[i].getColor().toString());
}

static void draw(Graphics g, ColoredDrawable[] cs) {
  for (int i=0; i<cs.length; i++) {
    g.setColor(cs[i].getColor());
    cs[i].draw(g);
  }
}
```

14 Exceptions, Checked and Unchecked

An *exception* is an object of an exception type: a subclass of class Throwable. It is used to signal and describe an abnormal situation during program execution. The evaluation of an expression or the execution of a statement may terminate abruptly by throwing an exception, either by executing a throw statement (section 12.6.5) or by executing a primitive operation, such as assignment to an array element, that may throw an exception.

A thrown exception may be caught in a dynamically enclosing try-catch statement (section 12.6.6). If the exception is not caught, then the entire program execution will be aborted, and information from the exception will be printed on the console. What is printed is determined by the exception's toString method.

There are two kinds of exception types: *checked* (those that must be declared in the *throws-clause* of a method or constructor; see section 9.8) and *unchecked* (those that need not be). If the execution of a method or constructor body can throw a checked exception of class E, then class E or a supertype of E must be declared in the *throws-clause* of the method or constructor.

The following table shows part of the exception class hierarchy.

Class	Status	Package
Throwable	checked	java.lang
Error	unchecked	java.lang
AssertionError	unchecked	java.lang
ExceptionInInitializerError	unchecked	java.lang
OutOfMemoryError	unchecked	java.lang
StackOverflowError	unchecked	java.lang
Exception	checked	java.lang
ClassNotFoundException	checked	java.lang
InterruptedException	checked	java.lang
IOException	checked	java.io
CharConversionException	checked	java.io
EOFException	checked	java.io
FileNotFoundException	checked	java.io
InterruptedIOException	checked	java.io
ObjectStreamException	checked	java.io
InvalidClassException	checked	java.io
NotSerializableException	checked	java.io
SyncFailedException	checked	java.io
UnsupportedEncodingException	checked	java.io
UTFDataFormatException	checked	java.io
RuntimeException	unchecked	java.lang
ArithmeticException	unchecked	java.lang
ArrayStoreException	unchecked	java.lang
ClassCastException	unchecked	java.lang
ConcurrentModificationException	unchecked	java.util
IllegalArgumentException	unchecked	java.lang
IllegalMonitorStateException	unchecked	java.lang
IllegalStateException	unchecked	java.lang
IndexOutOfBoundsException	unchecked	java.lang
ArrayIndexOutOfBoundsException	unchecked	java.lang
StringIndexOutOfBoundsException	unchecked	java.lang
NegativeArraySizeException	unchecked	java.util
NoSuchElementException	unchecked	java.util
NullPointerException	unchecked	java.lang
UnsupportedOperationException	unchecked	java.lang

Example 73 Declaring a Checked Exception Class
This is the class of exceptions thrown by method wdayno4 (example 65). Passing a string to the constructor of the superclass (that is, class Exception) causes method toString to append that string to the name of the exception.

```
class WeekdayException extends Exception {
  public WeekdayException(String wday) {
    super("Illegal weekday: " + wday);
  }
}
```

Example 74 All Paths Through a try-catch-finally Statement
To exercise all 18 paths through the try-catch-finally statement (section 12.6.6) in method m in the following program, run it with each of these command line arguments: 101 102 103 201 202 203 301 302 303 411 412 413 421 422 423 431 432 433. The try clause terminates normally on arguments 1*yz*, exits by return on 2*yz*, and throws an exception on 3*yz* and 4*yz*. The catch clause ignores exceptions thrown on 3*yz* but catches those thrown on 4*yz*; the catch clause terminates normally on 41*z*, exits by return on 42*z*, and throws an exception on 43*z*. The finally clause terminates normally on *xy*1, exits by return on *xy*2, and throws an exception on *xy*3.

Exits by break and continue statements are handled similarly to return; a more involved example could be constructed to illustrate their interaction.

```
class TryCatchFinally {
  public static void main(String[] args) throws Exception
  { System.out.println(m(Integer.parseInt(args[0]))); }

  static String m(int a) throws Exception {
    try {
      System.out.print("try ... ");
      if (a/100 == 2) return "returned from try";
      if (a/100 == 3) throw new Exception("thrown by try");
      if (a/100 == 4) throw new RuntimeException("thrown by try");
    } catch (RuntimeException x) {
      System.out.print("catch ... ");
      if (a/10%10 == 2) return "returned from catch";
      if (a/10%10 == 3) throw new Exception("thrown by catch");
    } finally {
      System.out.println("finally");
      if (a%10 == 2) return "returned from finally";
      if (a%10 == 3) throw new Exception("thrown by finally");
    }
    return "terminated normally with " + a;
  }
}
```

15 Threads, Concurrent Execution, and Synchronization

15.1 Threads and Concurrent Execution

The preceding chapters described sequential program execution, in which expressions are evaluated and state-ments are executed one after the other: they considered only a single thread of execution, where a *thread* is an independent sequential activity. A Java program may execute several threads concurrently, that is, potentially overlapping in time. For instance, one part of a program may continue computing while another part is blocked waiting for input (example 75).

A thread is created and controlled using an object of the Thread class found in the package `java.lang`. A thread executes the method `public void run()` in an object of a class implementing the Runnable inter-face, also found in package `java.lang`. To every thread (independent sequential activity) there is a unique controlling Thread object, so the two are often thought of as being identical.

One way to create and run a thread is to declare a class U as a subclass of Thread, overwriting its (trivial) run method. Then create an object u of class U and call `u.start()`. This will enable the thread to execute `u.run()` concurrently with other threads (example 75).

Alternatively, declare a class C that implements Runnable, create an object o of that class, create a thread object `u = new Thread(o)` from o, and execute `u.start()`. This will enable the thread to execute `o.run()` concurrently with other threads (example 79).

Threads can communicate with each other via shared state, namely, by using and assigning static fields, nonstatic fields, array elements, and pipes (section 21.15). By the design of Java, threads cannot use local variables and method parameters for communication.

States and State Transitions of a Thread

A thread is alive if it has been started and has not died. A thread dies by exiting its `run()` method, either by returning or by throwing an exception. A live thread is in one of the states Enabled (ready to run), Running (actually executing), Sleeping (waiting for a timeout), Joining (waiting for another thread to die), Locking (trying to obtain the lock on object o), or Waiting (for notification on object o). The thread state transitions are shown in the following table and the figure on the facing page:

From State	To State	Reason for Transition
Enabled	Running	System schedules thread for execution
Running	Enabled	System preempts thread and schedules another one
	Enabled	Thread executes `yield()`
	Waiting	Thread executes `o.wait()`, releasing lock on o
	Locking	Thread attempts to execute `synchronized (o) { ... }`
	Sleeping	Thread executes `sleep()`
	Joining	Thread executes `u.join()`
	Dead	Thread exited `run()` by returning or by throwing an exception
Sleeping	Enabled	Sleeping period expired
	Enabled	Thread was interrupted; throws InterruptedException when run
Joining	Enabled	Thread u being joined died, or join timed out
	Enabled	Thread was interrupted; throws InterruptedException when run
Waiting	Locking	Another thread executed `o.notify()` or `o.notifyAll()`
	Locking	Wait for lock on o timed out
	Locking	Thread was interrupted; throws InterruptedException when run
Locking	Enabled	Lock on o became available and was given to this thread

Example 75 Multiple Threads
The main program creates a new thread, binds it to u, and starts it. Now two threads are executing concurrently: one executes main, and another executes run. While the main method is blocked waiting for keyboard input, the new thread keeps incrementing i. The new thread executes yield() to make sure that the other thread is allowed to run (when not blocked).

```
class Incrementer extends Thread {
  public int i;
  public void run() {
    for (;;) {                                 // Forever
      i++;                                     //    increment i
      yield();
    }
} }

class ThreadDemo {
  public static void main(String[] args) throws IOException {
    Incrementer u = new Incrementer();
    u.start();
    System.out.println("Repeatedly press Enter to get the current value of i:");
    for (;;) {
      System.in.read();                        // Wait for keyboard input
      System.out.println(u.i);
} } }
```

States and state transitions of a thread.   A thread's transition from one state to another may be caused by a method call performed by the thread itself (shown in the monospace font), by a method call possibly performed by another thread (shown in the *slanted monospace* font); and by timeouts and other actions.

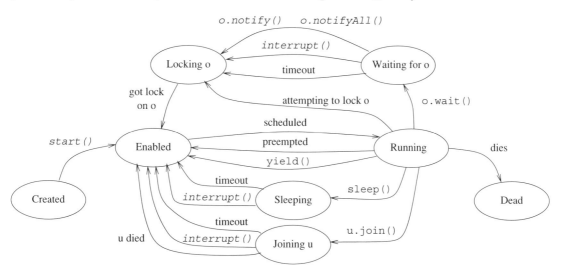

15.2   Locks and the `synchronized` Statement

Concurrent threads are executed independently. Therefore, when multiple concurrent threads access the same fields or array elements, there is considerable risk of creating an inconsistent state (example 77). To avoid this, threads may synchronize the access to shared state, such as objects and arrays. A single *lock* is associated with every object, array, and class. A lock can be held by at most one thread at a time. A thread may explicitly request the lock on an object or array by executing a `synchronized` statement, which has this form:

> `synchronized` (*expression*)
>   *block-statement*

The *expression* must have reference type. The *expression* must evaluate to a non-`null` reference o; otherwise a NullPointerException is thrown. After the evaluation of the *expression*, the thread becomes Locking on object o; see the figure on the previous page. When the thread obtains the lock on object o (if ever), the thread becomes Enabled, and may become Running so the *block-statement* is executed. When the *block-statement* terminates or is exited by `return` or `break` or `continue` or by throwing an exception, then the lock on o is released.

A `synchronized` nonstatic method declaration (section 9.8) is shorthand for a method whose body has the form

> `synchronized (this)`
>   *method-body*

That is, the thread will execute the method body only when it has obtained the lock on the current object. It will release the lock when it leaves the method body.

A `synchronized` static method declaration (section 9.8) in class C is shorthand for a method whose body has the form

> `synchronized (C.class)`
>   *method-body*

That is, the thread will execute the method body only when it has obtained the lock on the object C.class, which is the unique object of class Class associated with the class C. It will hold the lock until it leaves the method body, and release it at that time.

Constructors and initializers cannot be synchronized.

Mutual exclusion is ensured only if *all* threads accessing a shared object lock it before use. For instance, if we add an unsynchronized method `roguetransfer` to a bank object (example 77), we can no longer be sure that a thread calling the synchronized method `transfer` has exclusive access to the bank object: any number of threads could be executing `roguetransfer` at the same time.

A *monitor* is an object whose fields are private and are manipulated only by synchronized methods of the object, so that all field access is subject to synchronization (example 78).

If a thread u needs to wait for some condition to become true, or for a resource to become available, it may temporarily release its lock on object o by calling `o.wait()`. The thread must hold the lock on object o, otherwise exception IllegalMonitorStateException is thrown. The thread u will be added to the *wait set* of o, that is, the set of threads waiting for notification on object o. This notification must come from another thread that has obtained the lock on o and that executes `o.notify()` or `o.notifyAll()`. The notifying thread does not release its lock on o. After being notified, u must obtain the lock on o again before it can proceed. Thus when the call to `wait` returns, thread u will hold the lock on o just as before the call (example 78).

For detailed rules governing the behavior of unsynchronized Java threads, see chapter 17 of the Java Language Specification [1].

Example 76 Mutual Exclusion

A Printer thread forever prints a (-) followed by a (/). If we create and run two concurrent printer threads using new Printer().start() and new Printer().start(), then only one of the threads can hold the lock on object mutex at a time, so no other symbols can be printed between (-) and (/) in one iteration of the for loop. Thus the program must print -/-/-/-/-/-/-/ and so on. However, if the synchronization is removed, it may print --//--/-/-//--// and so on. The call Util.pause(n) pauses the thread for 200 ms, whereas Util.pause(100,300) pauses it between 100 and 300 ms. This is done only to make the inherent nondeterminacy of unsynchronized concurrency more easily observable.

```
class Printer extends Thread {
  static Object mutex = new Object();
  public void run() {
    for (;;) {
      synchronized (mutex) {
        System.out.print("-");
        Util.pause(100,300);
        System.out.print("/");
      }
      Util.pause(200);
} } }
```

Example 77 Synchronized Methods in an Object

The Bank object here has two accounts. Money is repeatedly being transferred from one account to the other by clerks. Clearly the total amount of money should remain constant (at 30 euro). This holds true when the transfer method is declared synchronized, because only one clerk can access the accounts at any one time. If the synchronized declaration is removed, the sum will differ from 30 most of the time, because one clerk is likely to overwrite the other's deposits and withdrawals.

```
class Bank {
  private int account1 = 10, account2 = 20;
  synchronized public void transfer(int amount) {
    int new1 = account1 - amount;
    Util.pause(10);
    account1 = new1; account2 = account2 + amount;
    System.out.println("Sum is " + (account1+account2));
} }

class Clerk extends Thread {
  private Bank bank;
  public Clerk(Bank bank) { this.bank = bank; }
  public void run() {
    for (;;) {                           // Forever
      bank.transfer(Util.random(-10, 10));  //   transfer money
      Util.pause(200, 300);                 //   then take a break
} } }

... Bank bank = new Bank();
... new Clerk(bank).start(); new Clerk(bank).start();
```

15.3   Operations on Threads

The current thread, whose state is Running, may call these methods among others. Further Thread methods are described in the Java class library documentation [3].

- `Thread.yield()` changes the state of the current thread from Running to Enabled, and thereby allows the system to schedule another Enabled thread, if any.
- `Thread.sleep(n)` sleeps for n milliseconds: the current thread becomes Sleeping and after n milliseconds becomes Enabled. May throw InterruptedException if the thread is interrupted while sleeping.
- `Thread.currentThread()` returns the current thread object.
- `Thread.interrupted()` returns and clears the *interrupted status* of the current thread: `true` if there has been no call to `Thread.interrupted()` and no InterruptedException thrown since the last interrupt; otherwise `false`.

Let u be a thread (an object of a subclass of Thread). Then

- `u.start()` changes the state of u to Enabled so that its `run` method will be called when a processor becomes available.
- `u.interrupt()` interrupts the thread u: if u is Running or Enabled or Locking, then its interrupted status is set to `true`. If u is Sleeping or Joining, it will become Enabled, and if it is Waiting, it will become Locking; in these cases u will throw InterruptedException when and if it becomes Running (and the interrupted status is set to `false`).
- `u.isInterrupted()` returns the interrupted status of u (and does not clear it).
- `u.join()` waits for thread u to die; may throw InterruptedException if the current thread is interrupted while waiting.
- `u.join(n)` works as `u.join()` but times out and returns after at most n milliseconds. There is no indication whether the call returned because of a timeout or because u died.

Operations on Locked Objects

A thread that holds the lock on an object o may call the following methods, inherited by o from class Object.

- `o.wait()` releases the lock on o, changes its own state to Waiting, and adds itself to the set of threads waiting for notification on o. When notified (if ever), the thread must obtain the lock on o, so when the call to `wait` returns, it again holds the lock on o. May throw InterruptedException if the thread is interrupted while waiting.
- `o.wait(n)` works like `o.wait()` except that the thread will change state to Locking after n milliseconds regardless of whether there has been a notification on o. There is no indication whether the state change was caused by a timeout or because of a notification.
- `o.notify()` chooses an arbitrary thread among the threads waiting for notification on o (if any) and changes its state to Locking. The chosen thread cannot actually obtain the lock on o until the current thread has released it.
- `o.notifyAll()` works like `o.notify()`, except that it changes the state to Locking for *all* threads waiting for notification on o.

Example 78 Producers and Consumers Communicating via a Monitor

A Buffer has room for one integer, and has a method `put` for storing into the buffer (if empty) and a method `get` for reading from the buffer (if nonempty); it is a monitor (section 15.2). A thread calling `get` must obtain the lock on the buffer. If it finds that the buffer is empty, it calls `wait` to (release the lock and) wait until something has been `put` into the buffer. If another thread calls `put` and thus `notify`, then the getting thread will start competing for the buffer lock again, and if it gets it, will continue executing. Here we have used a `synchronized` statement in the method body (instead of making the method `synchronized`, as is normal for a monitor) to emphasize that synchronization, `wait`, and `notify` all work on the same buffer object `this`.

```
class Buffer {
  private int contents;
  private boolean empty = true;
  public int get() {
    synchronized (this) {
      while (empty)
        try { this.wait(); } catch (InterruptedException x) {};
      empty = true;
      this.notify();
      return contents;
  } }
  public void put(int v) {
    synchronized (this) {
      while (!empty)
        try { this.wait(); } catch (InterruptedException x) {};
      empty = false;
      contents = v;
      this.notify();
  } }
}
```

Example 79 Graphic Animation Using the Runnable Interface

Class AnimatedCanvas here is a subclass of Canvas and so cannot be a subclass of Thread also. Instead it declares a `run` method and implements the Runnable interface. The constructor creates a Thread object u from the AnimatedCanvas object `this` and then starts the thread. The new thread executes the `run` method, which repeatedly sleeps and repaints, thus creating an animation.

```
class AnimatedCanvas extends Canvas implements Runnable {
  AnimatedCanvas() { Thread u = new Thread(this); u.start(); }

  public void run() {                        // From interface Runnable
    for (;;) { // Forever sleep and repaint
      try { Thread.sleep(100); } catch (InterruptedException e) { }
      ...
      repaint();
    }
  }

  public void paint(Graphics g) { ... }      // From class Canvas
  ...
}
```

16   Compilation, Source Files, Class Names, and Class Files

A *Java program* consists of one or more *source files* (with file name suffix .java). A source file may contain one or more class or interface declarations. A source file can contain at most one declaration of a top-level public class or interface, which must then have the same name as the file (minus the file name suffix). A source file myprog.java is compiled to Java class files (with file name suffix .class) by a Java compiler:

```
javac myprog.java
```

This creates one class file for each class or interface declared in the source file myprog.java. A class or interface C declared in a top-level declaration produces a class file called C.class. A nested class or interface D declared inside class C produces a class file called C$D.class. A local class D declared inside a method in class C produces a class file called C1D.class or similar.

A Java class C that declares the method public static void main(String[] args) can be executed using the Java run-time system java by typing a command line of the form

```
java C arg1 arg2 ...
```

This will execute the body of method main with the command line arguments *arg*1, *arg*2, ... bound to the array elements args[0], args[1], ... inside the method main (examples 6 and 84).

17   Packages and Jar Files

Java source files may be organized in *packages*. Every source file in package p must begin with the declaration

```
package p;
```

and must be stored in a subdirectory called p. A class declared in a source file with no package declaration belongs to the anonymous *default package*. A source file not belonging to package p may refer to class C from package p by using the qualified name p.C, in which the class name C is prefixed by the package name. To avoid using the package name prefix, the source file may begin with an import declaration (possibly following a package declaration) of one of these forms:

```
import p.C;
import p.*;
```

The former allows C to be used unqualified, without the package name, and the latter allows all accessible classes and interfaces in package p to be used unqualified. The Java class library package java.lang is implicitly imported into all source files, as if by import java.lang.*, so all java.lang classes can be used unqualified in Java source files. Note that java.lang is a composite package name, so class java.lang.String is declared in file java/lang/String.java.

The files in p and its subdirectories can be put into a *jar file* called p.jar using the program jar:

```
jar vcf p.jar p
```

The packages in a jar file can be made available to other Java programs by moving the file to the directory /usr/java/j2sdk1.4.0/jre/lib/ext or similar under Unix, or to the directory c:\jdk1.4\jre\lib\ext or similar under MS Windows. The jar file may contain more than one package; it need only contain class files (not source files); and its name is not significant.

Example 80 The Vessel Hierarchy as a Package
The package `vessel` here contains part of the vessel hierarchy (example 19). The fields in classes Tank and Barrel are `final`, so they cannot be modified after object creation. They are `protected`, so they are accessible in subclasses declared outside the `vessel` package, as shown in file `Usevessels.java`, which is in the anonymous default package, not in the `vessel` package.

The file `vessel/Vessel.java`

```
package vessel;
public abstract class Vessel {
  private double contents;
  public abstract double capacity();
  public final void fill(double amount)
  { contents = Math.min(contents + amount, capacity()); }
  public final double getContents() { return contents; }
}
```

The file `vessel/Tank.java`

```
package vessel;
public class Tank extends Vessel {
  protected final double length, width, height;
  public Tank(double l, double w, double h) { length = l; width = w; height = h; }
  public double capacity() { return length * width * height; }
  public String toString()
  { return "tank (l,w,h) = (" + length + ", " + width + ", " + height + ")"; }
}
```

The file `vessel/Barrel.java`

```
package vessel;
public class Barrel extends Vessel {
  protected final double radius, height;
  public Barrel(double r, double h) { radius = r; height = h; }
  public double capacity() { return height * Math.PI * radius * radius; }
  public String toString() { return "barrel (r, h) = (" + radius + ", " + height + ")"; }
}
```

The file `Usevessels.java`

Subclass Cube of class Tank may access the field `length` because that field is declared `protected` in Tank above. The `main` method is unmodified from example 20.

```
import vessel.*;
class Cube extends Tank {
  public Cube(double side) { super(side, side, side); }
  public String toString() { return "cube (s) = (" + length + ")"; }
}
class Usevessels {
  public static void main(String[] args) { ... }
}
```

18   Mathematical Functions

Class Math provides static methods to compute standard mathematical functions. Floating-point numbers (double and float) include positive and negative infinities as well as nonnumbers (NaN), following the IEEE754 standard [6]. There is also a distinction between positive zero and negative zero, ignored here.

The Math methods return nonnumbers (NaN) when applied to illegal arguments, and return infinities in case of overflow; they do not throw exceptions. Also, the methods return NaN when applied to NaN arguments, except where noted, and behave sensibly when applied to positive or negative infinities.

Angles are given and returned in radians, not degrees. Methods that round to nearest integer will round to the nearest even integer in case of a tie.

The methods abs, min, and max are overloaded on float, int, and long arguments also.

- static double E is the constant $e \approx 2.71828$, the base of the natural logarithm.
- static double PI is the constant $\pi \approx 3.14159$, the circumference of a circle with diameter 1.
- static double abs(double x) is the absolute value: x if x>=0, and -x if x<0.
- static double acos(double x) is the arc cosine of x, in the range $[0, \pi]$, for -1<=x<=1.
- static double asin(double x) is the arc sine of x, in the range $[-\pi/2, \pi/2]$, for -1<=x<=1.
- static double atan(double x) is the arc tangent of x, in the range $[-\pi/2, \pi/2]$.
- static double atan2(double y, double x) is the arc tangent of y/x in the quadrant of the point (x, y), in the range $]-\pi, \pi]$. When x is 0, the result is $\pi/2$ with the same sign as y.
- static double ceil(double x) is the smallest integral double value >=x.
- static double cos(double x) is the cosine of x, in the range $[-1, 1]$.
- static double exp(double x) is the exponential of x, that is, e to the power x.
- static double floor(double x) is the largest integral double value <=x.
- static double IEEEremainder(double x, double y) is the remainder of x/y, that is, x-y*n, where n is the mathematical integer closest to x/y.
- static double log(double x) is the natural logarithm (to base e) of x, for x>=0.
- static double max(double x, double y) is the greatest of x and y.
- static double min(double x, double y) is the smallest of x and y.
- static double pow(double x, double y) is x to the power y, that is, x^y. If y is 0, then the result is 1.0. If y is 1, then the result is x. If x<0 and y is not integral, then the result is NaN.
- static double random() returns a uniformly distributed pseudo-random number in $[0, 1[$.
- static double rint(double x) is the integral double value that is closest to x.
- static long round(double x) is the long value that is closest to x.
- static int round(float x) is the int value that is closest to x.
- static double sin(double x) is the sine of x radians.
- static double sqrt(double x) is the positive square root of x, for x>=0.
- static double tan(double x) is the tangent of x radians.
- static double toDegrees(double r) is the number of degrees corresponding to r radians.
- static double toRadians(double d) is the number of radians corresponding to d degrees.

Example 81 Floating-Point Factorial
This method computes the factorial function $n! = 1 \cdot 2 \cdot 3 \cdots (n-1) \cdot n$ using logarithms.

```
static double fact(int n) {
  double res = 0.0;
  for (int i=1; i<=n; i++)
    res += Math.log(i);
  return Math.exp(res);
}
```

Example 82 Generating Gaussian Pseudo-Random Numbers
This example uses the Box-Muller transformation to generate N Gaussian, or normally distributed, pseudo-random numbers with mean 0 and standard deviation 1.

```
for (int i=0; i<N; i+=2) {
  double x1 = Math.random(), x2 = Math.random();
  print(Math.sqrt(-2 * Math.log(x1)) * Math.cos(2 * Math.PI * x2));
  print(Math.sqrt(-2 * Math.log(x1)) * Math.sin(2 * Math.PI * x2));
}
```

Example 83 Mathematical Functions: Infinities, NaNs, and Special Cases

```
print("Illegal arguments, NaN results:");
print(Math.sqrt(-1));            // NaN
print(Math.log(-1));            // NaN
print(Math.pow(-1, 2.5));       // NaN
print(Math.acos(1.1));          // NaN
print("Infinite results:");
print(Math.log(0));            // -Infinity
print(Math.pow(0, -1));         // Infinity
print(Math.exp(1000.0));        // Infinity (overflow)
print("Infinite arguments:");
double infinity = Double.POSITIVE_INFINITY;
print(Math.sqrt(infinity));     // Infinity
print(Math.log(infinity));      // Infinity
print(Math.exp(-infinity));     // 0.0
print("NaN arguments and special cases:");
double nan = Math.log(-1);
print(Math.sqrt(nan));          // NaN
print(Math.pow(nan, 0));        // 1.0 (special case)
print(Math.pow(0, 0));          // 1.0 (special case)
print(Math.round(nan));         // 0   (special case)
print(Math.round(1E50));        // 9223372036854775807 (Long.MAX_VALUE)
// For all (x, y) except (0.0, 0.0):
// sign(cos(atan2(y, x))) == sign(x) && sign(sin(atan2(y, x))) == sign(y)
for (double x=-100; x<=100; x+=0.125) {
  for (double y=-100; y<=100; y+=0.125) {
    double r = Math.atan2(y, x);
    if (!(sign(Math.cos(r))==sign(x) && sign(Math.sin(r))==sign(y)))
      print("x = " + x + "; y = " + y);
  }
}
```

19   String Buffers

A String object s1, once created, cannot be modified. Using s1 + s2 one can append another string s2 to s1, but that creates a new string object, copying all the characters from s1 and s2; there is no way to extend s1 itself by appending more characters to it. Thus to concatenate *n* strings each of length *k* by repeated string concatenation (+), we copy $k + 2k + 3k + \cdots + nk - kn(n+1)/2$ characters, and the time required to do this is proportional to kn^2, which grows rapidly as *n* grows.

String buffers, which are objects of the predefined class StringBuffer, provide extensible and modifiable strings. Characters can be appended to a string buffer without copying those characters already in the string buffer; the string buffer is automatically and efficiently extended as needed. To concatenate *n* strings each of length *k* using a string buffer requires only time proportional to *kn*, considerably faster than kn^2 for large *n*. Thus to gradually build a string, use a string buffer. This is needed only for repeated concatenation in a loop, as in example 6. The expression s1 + $\cdots$ + sn is efficient; it actually means
new StringBuffer().append(s1).$\cdots$.append(sn).toString().

Let sb be a StringBuffer, s a String, and v an expression of any type. Then

- new StringBuffer() creates a new empty string buffer.

- sb.append(v) appends the string representation of the value v to the string buffer, converting v by String.valueOf(v), see chapter 7. Extends sb as needed. Returns sb.

- sb.charAt(int i) returns character number i (counting from zero) in the string buffer. Throws StringIndexOutOfBoundsException if i<0 or i>=sb.length().

- sb.delete(from, to) deletes the characters with index from..(to-1) from the string buffer, reducing its length by to-from characters. Throws StringIndexOutOfBoundsException if from<0 or from>to or to>sb.length(). Returns sb.

- sb.insert(from, v) inserts the string representation of v obtained by String.valueOf(v) into the string buffer, starting at position from, extending sb as needed. Returns sb. Throws StringIndexOutOfBoundsException if from<0 or from>sb.length().

- sb.length() of type int is the length of sb, that is, the number of characters currently in sb.

- sb.replace(from, to, s) replaces the characters with index from..(to-1) in the string buffer by the string s, extending sb if needed. Throws StringIndexOutOfBoundsException if from<0 or from>to or from>sb.length(). Returns sb.

- sb.reverse() reverses the character sequence in the string buffer. Returns sb.

- sb.setCharAt(i, c) sets the character at index i to c. Throws StringIndexOutOfBoundsException if i<0 or i>=sb.length().

- sb.toString() of type String is a new string containing the characters currently in sb.

- Method append is fast, but delete, insert, and replace may be slow when they need to move large parts of the string buffer — when from and to are much smaller than length().

- Operations on a StringBuffer object are thread-safe: several concurrent threads (chapter 15) can modify the same string buffer without making its internal state inconsistent.

- More StringBuffer methods are described in the Java class library documentation [3].

Example 84 Efficiently Concatenating All Command Line Arguments
When there are many (more than 50) command line arguments, this is much faster than example 6.

```
public static void main(String[] args) {
  StringBuffer res = new StringBuffer();
  for (int i=0; i<args.length; i++)
    res.append(args[i]);
  System.out.println(res.toString());
}
```

Example 85 Replacing Occurrences of a Character by a String
To replace occurrences of character c1 with the string s2 in string s, it is best to use a string buffer for the result, since the size of the resulting string is not known in advance. This works well also when replacing a character c1 with another character c2, but in that case the length of the result is known in advance (it equals the length of s) and one can use a character array instead (example 13). Solving this problem by repeated string concatenation (using res += s2) would be very slow.

```
static String replaceCharString(String s, char c1, String s2) {
  StringBuffer res = new StringBuffer();
  for (int i=0; i<s.length(); i++)
    if (s.charAt(i) == c1)
      res.append(s2);
    else
      res.append(s.charAt(i));
  return res.toString();
}
```

Example 86 Inefficiently Replacing Occurrences of a Character by a String
The problem from example 85 can also be solved by destructively modifying a string buffer with replace. However, repeatedly using replace is inefficient: for a string of 200,000 random characters this method is approximately 100 times slower than the one in example 85.

```
static void replaceCharString(StringBuffer sb, char c1, String s2) {
  int i = 0;                            // Inefficient
  while (i < sb.length()) {             // Inefficient
    if (sb.charAt(i) == c1) {           // Inefficient
      sb.replace(i, i+1, s2);           // Inefficient
      i += s2.length();                 // Inefficient
    } else                              // Inefficient
      i += 1;                           // Inefficient
} }                                     // Inefficient
```

Example 87 Padding a String to a Given Width
A string s may be padded with spaces to make sure that it has a certain minimum size width. This is useful for aligning numbers into columns when using a fixed-pitch font (example 103).

```
static String padLeft(String s, int width) {
  StringBuffer res = new StringBuffer();
  for (int i=width-s.length(); i>0; i--)
    res.append(' ');
  return res.append(s).toString();
}
```

20   Collections and Maps

The Java class library package `java.util` provides collection classes and map classes:

- A *collection*, described by interface Collection (section 20.1), is used to group and handle many distinct *elements* as a whole.

- A *list*, described by interface List (section 20.2), is a collection whose elements can be traversed in insertion order. Implemented by the classes LinkedList (for linked lists, double-ended queues, and stacks) and ArrayList (for dynamically extensible arrays and stacks).

- A *set*, described by interface Set (section 20.3), is a collection that cannot contain duplicate elements. Implemented by the classes HashSet and LinkedHashSet.

  A *sorted set*, described by interface SortedSet (section 20.4), is a set whose elements are ordered: either the elements implement method `compareTo` specified by interface Comparable, or the set's ordering is given explicitly by an object of type Comparator (section 20.8). Implemented by class TreeSet.

- A *map*, described by interface Map (section 20.5), represents a mapping from a key to at most one value for each key. Implemented by the classes HashMap, IdentityHashMap, and LinkedHashMap.

  A *sorted map*, described by interface SortedMap (section 20.6), is a map whose keys are ordered, as for SortedSet. Implemented by class TreeMap.

The relations between the standard interfaces and concrete implementation classes, and the intermediate abstract classes, are shown in the following figure. User-defined implementation classes can be conveniently defined as subclasses of the abstract classes, see the Java class library documentation on package `java.util` [3]. Solid arrows denote the subinterface and subclass relations, and dashed arrows indicate the "implements" relation between a class and an interface.

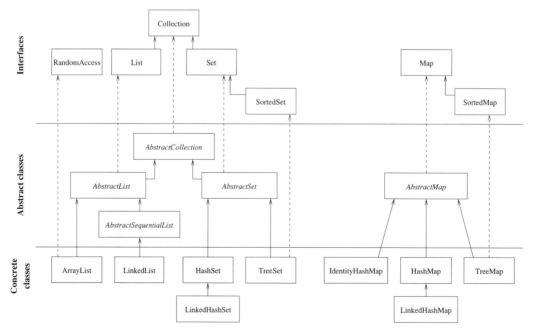

Example 88 Using the Concrete Collection and Map Classes
Here we create instances of five concrete collection classes and add some String elements to them. For each collection, we call method `traverse` in example 91 to print its elements.

We also create instances of three concrete map classes and add some entries to them. For each map, we call `traverse` separately on the set of keys and the collection of values of that map.

Note that TreeSet, which implements SortedSet, guarantees that the elements will be traversed in the order specified by the `compareTo` method (section 20.8) of the elements, and LinkedHashSet guarantees that the elements will be traversed in insertion order, whereas HashSet provides no such guarantee. Similarly, a TreeMap guarantees traversal in key order, and LinkedHashMap guarantees traversal in key insertion order, whereas HashMap does not guarantee any particular order.

```java
import java.util.*;

class CollectionAll {
  public static void main(String[] args) {
    List /* of String */ list1 = new LinkedList();
    list1.add("list"); list1.add("dup"); list1.add("x"); list1.add("dup");
    traverse(list1);                    // Must print: list dup x dup
    List /* of String */ list2 = new ArrayList();
    list2.add("list"); list2.add("dup"); list2.add("x"); list2.add("dup");
    traverse(list2);                    // Must print: list dup x dup
    Set /* of String */ set1 = new HashSet();
    set1.add("set"); set1.add("dup"); set1.add("x"); set1.add("dup");
    traverse(set1);                     // May print:  x dup set
    SortedSet /* of String */ set2 = new TreeSet();
    set2.add("set"); set2.add("dup"); set2.add("x"); set2.add("dup");
    traverse(set2);                     // Must print: dup set x
    LinkedHashSet /* of String */ set3 = new LinkedHashSet();
    set3.add("set"); set3.add("dup"); set3.add("x"); set3.add("dup");
    traverse(set3);                     // Must print: set dup x
    Map /* from String to String */ m1 = new HashMap();
    m1.put("map", "J"); m1.put("dup", "K"); m1.put("x", "M"); m1.put("dup", "L");
    traverse(m1.keySet());             // May print:  x dup map
    traverse(m1.values());            // May print:  M L J
    SortedMap /* from String to String */ m2 = new TreeMap();
    m2.put("map", "J"); m2.put("dup", "K"); m2.put("x", "M"); m2.put("dup", "L");
    traverse(m2.keySet());             // Must print: dup map x
    traverse(m2.values());            // Must print: L J M
    LinkedHashMap /* from String to String */ m3 = new LinkedHashMap();
    m3.put("map", "J"); m3.put("dup", "K"); m3.put("x", "M"); m3.put("dup", "L");
    traverse(m3.keySet());             // Must print: map dup x
    traverse(m3.values());            // Must print: J L M
  }

  static void traverse(Collection coll) { ... }
}
```

20.1   The Collection Interface

The Collection interface describes the following methods:

- `boolean add(Object o)` adds element o to the collection; returns `true` if the element was added, `false` if the collection disallows duplicates and contains an element equal to o already.
- `boolean addAll(Collection coll)` adds all elements of `coll` to the collection; returns `true` if any element was added.
- `void clear()` removes all elements from the collection.
- `boolean contains(Object o)` returns `true` if any element of the collection equals o.
- `boolean containsAll(Collection coll)` returns `true` if the collection contains all elements of `coll`.
- `boolean isEmpty()` returns `true` if the collection has no elements.
- `Iterator iterator()` returns an iterator (section 20.7) over the elements of the collection.
- `boolean remove(Object o)` removes a single instance of element o from the collection; returns `true` if the collection contained such an element.
- `boolean removeAll(Collection coll)` removes all those elements that are also in `coll`; returns `true` if any element was removed. No element of the resulting collection equals an element of `coll`.
- `boolean retainAll(Collection coll)` retains only those elements that are also in `coll`; returns `true` if any element was removed.
- `int size()` returns the number of elements in the collection.
- `Object[] toArray()` returns an array of all the elements of the collection.
- `Object[] toArray(Object[] a)` works like the preceding, but the array's element type is that of a.

The elements of a collection, and the keys and values of a map, must be objects or arrays. For elements of primitive type, such as int, use a wrapper class such as `Integer` (section 5.1).

When inserting an element of class C into a collection, it is cast to type Object, and when extracting it again, it is (usually) cast back to type C. These casts are checked only at run-time, not by the compiler, so programs that use collections are essentially *dynamically typed*: the Java compiler will not prevent you from adding a `String` to a set of `Integer` objects. For this reason it is recommended to document the intended collection element types by program comments, and to use explicit casts (section 11.12) whenever an element is extracted from a collection or map.

A *view* of a collection co1 is a another collection co2 that refers to the same underlying data structure. As a consequence, modifications to co1 affect co2, and modifications to co2 affect co1.

An *unmodifiable collection* does not admit modification: the operations add, clear, remove, set, and so on throw UnsupportedOperationException. The utility class Collections (section 20.9) provides static methods to create an unmodifiable view of a given collection.

A *synchronized collection* is thread-safe: several concurrent threads can safely access and modify it. For efficiency, the standard collection classes are not synchronized, so concurrent modification of a collection may make its internal state inconsistent. The utility class Collections (section 20.9) provides static methods to create a synchronized view of a given collection. All concurrent access to a collection should go through its synchronized view. An iterator (section 20.7) obtained from a synchronized collection coll does not automatically provide synchronized iteration; one must use `synchronized (coll) { ... }` to explicitly ensure exclusive access to the collection during the execution of the block `{ ... }` that performs the iteration.

20.2   The List Interface and the LinkedList and ArrayList Implementations

The List interface extends the Collection interface with operations for position-based access using indexes $0, 1, 2, \ldots$ and gives more precise specifications of some methods:

- `void add(int i, Object o)` adds element o at position i, increasing the index of any element to the right by 1. Throws IndexOutOfBoundsException if `i<0` or `i>size()`.
- `boolean addAll(int i, Collection coll)` adds all elements of `coll` to the list, starting at position i; returns `true` if any element was added. Throws IndexOutOfBoundsException if `i<0` or `i>size()`.
- `boolean equals(Object o)` returns `true` if o is a List with equal elements in the same order.
- `Object get(int i)` returns the element at position i; throws IndexOutOfBoundsException if `i<0` or `i>=size()`.
- `int hashCode()` returns the hash code of the list, which is a function of the hash codes of the elements and their order in the list.
- `int indexOf(Object o)` returns the least index i for which the element at position i equals o; returns -1 if the list does not contain such an element.
- `int lastIndexOf(Object o)` returns the greatest index i for which the element at position i equals o; returns -1 if the list does not contain such an element.
- `ListIterator listIterator()` returns a list iterator, which is a bidirectional iterator.
- `Object remove(int i)` removes the element at position i and returns it;
  throws IndexOutOfBoundsException if `i<0` or `i>=size()`.
- `Object set(int i, Object o)` sets the element at position i to o and returns the element previously at position i; throws IndexOutOfBoundsException if `i<0` or `i>=size()`.
- `List subList(int from, int to)` returns a list of the elements at positions `from..(to-1)`, as a view of the underlying list. Throws IndexOutOfBoundsException if `from<0` or `from>to` or `to>size()`.

The LinkedList class implements all the operations described by the List interface and has the following constructors. The implementation is a doubly linked list, so elements can be accessed, added, and removed efficiently at either end of the list. It therefore provides additional methods for position-based `get`, `add`, and `remove` called `addFirst`, `addLast`, `getFirst`, `getLast`, `removeFirst`, and `removeLast`. The latter four throw NoSuchElementException if the list is empty.

- `LinkedList()` creates a new empty LinkedList.
- `LinkedList(Collection coll)` creates a new LinkedList of the elements provided by `coll`'s iterator.

The ArrayList class implements all the operations described by the List interface and has the following constructors. The implementation uses an underlying array (expanded as needed to hold the elements), which permits efficient position-based access anywhere in the list. Class ArrayList implements the RandomAccess interface just to indicate that element access by index is guaranteed to be fast, in contrast to LinkedList. The ArrayList class provides all the functionality originally provided by the Vector class (which is a subclass of AbstractList and implements List and RandomAccess).

- `ArrayList()` creates a new empty list.
- `ArrayList(Collection coll)` creates a new ArrayList of the elements provided by `coll`'s iterator.

20.3   The Set Interface and the HashSet and LinkedHashSet Implementations

The Set interface describes the same methods as the Collection interface. The methods add and addAll must make sure that a set contains no duplicates: no two equal elements and at most one null element. Also, the methods equals and hashCode have more precise specifications for Set objects:

- boolean equals(Object o) returns true if o is a Set with the same number of elements, and every element of o is also in this set.
- int hashCode() returns the hash code of the set: the sum of the hash codes of its non-null elements.

For Set arguments, addAll computes set union, containsAll computes set inclusion, removeAll computes set difference, and retainAll computes set intersection (example 97).

The HashSet class implements the Set interface and has the following constructors. Operations on a HashSet rely on the equals and hashCode methods of the element objects.

- HashSet() creates an empty set.
- HashSet(Collection coll) creates a set containing the elements of coll, without duplicates.

The LinkedHashSet class is a subclass of HashSet and works the same way but additionally guarantees that its iterator traverses the elements in insertion order (rather than the unpredictable order provided by HashSet). It was introduced in Java 2, version 1.4.

20.4   The SortedSet Interface and the TreeSet Implementation

The SortedSet interface extends the Set interface. Operations on a SortedSet rely on the natural ordering of the elements defined by their compareTo method, or on an explicit Comparator object provided when the set was created (section 20.8), as for TreeSet below.

- Comparator comparator() returns the Comparator associated with this sorted set, or null if it uses the natural ordering (section 20.8) of the elements.
- Object first() returns the least element; throws NoSuchElementException if set is empty.
- SortedSet headSet(Object to) returns the set of all elements strictly less than to. The resulting set is a view of the underlying set.
- Object last() returns the greatest element; throws NoSuchElementException if set is empty.
- SortedSet subSet(Object from, Object to) returns the set of all elements greater than or equal to from and strictly less than to. The resulting set is a view of the underlying set.
- SortedSet tailSet(Object from) returns the set of all elements greater than or equal to from. The resulting set is a view of the underlying set.

The TreeSet class implements the SortedSet interface and has the following constructors. The implementation uses balanced binary trees, so all operations are guaranteed to be efficient.

- TreeSet() creates an empty set, ordering elements using their compareTo method.
- TreeSet(Collection coll) creates a set containing the elements of coll, without duplicates, ordering elements using their compareTo method.
- TreeSet(Comparator cmp) creates an empty set, ordering elements using cmp.
- TreeSet(SortedSet s) creates a set containing the elements of s, ordering elements as in s.

20.5   The Map Interface and the HashMap Implementation

The Map interface describes the following methods. A map can be considered a collection of entries, where an *entry* is a pair (k,v) of a key k and a value v, both of which must be objects or arrays. Thus to use values of primitive type, such as int, as keys or values, one must use the corresponding wrapper class, such as Integer (section 5.1). A map can contain no two entries with the same key.

- void clear() removes all entries from this map.
- boolean containsKey(Object k) returns true if the map has an entry with key k.
- boolean containsValue(Object v) returns true if the map has an entry with value v.
- Set entrySet() returns a set view of the map's entries; each entry has type Map.Entry (see below).
- boolean equals(Object o) returns true if o is a Map with the same entry set.
- Object get(Object k) returns the value v in the entry (k, v) with key k, if any; otherwise null.
- int hashCode() returns the hash code for the map, computed as the sum of the hash codes of the entries returned by entrySet().
- boolean isEmpty() returns true if this map contains no entries, that is, size() is zero.
- Set keySet() returns a set view of the keys in the map.
- Object put(Object k, Object v) modifies the map so that it contains the entry (k, v); returns the value previously associated with key k, if any; else returns null.
- void putAll(Map map) copies all entries from map to this map.
- Object remove(Object k) removes the entry for key k from the map, if any; returns the value previously associated with k, if any; else returns null.
- int size() returns the number of entries, which equals the number of keys, in the map.
- Collection values() returns a collection view of the values in the map.

The Map.Entry interface (example 92) describes operations on map entries:

- Object getKey() returns the key in this entry.
- Object getValue() returns the value in this entry.

The HashMap class implements the Map interface and has the following constructors. Operations on a HashMap rely on the equals and hashCode methods of the key objects.

- HashMap() creates an empty HashMap.
- HashMap(Map map) creates a HashMap containing the entries map.

The LinkedHashMap class is a subclass of HashMap and works the same way but additionally guarantees that its iterator traverses the entries in key insertion order (rather than the unpredictable order provided by HashMap). It was introduced in Java 2, version 1.4.

The IdentityHashMap class implements the Map interface but compares keys using reference equality (==) instead of the equals method. It was introduced in Java 2, version 1.4.

20.6   The SortedMap Interface and the TreeMap Implementation

The SortedMap interface extends the Map interface. Operations on a SortedMap rely on the natural ordering of the keys defined by their `compareTo` method or on an explicit Comparator object provided when the map was created (section 20.8), as for TreeMap below.

- `Comparator comparator()` returns the Comparator associated with this sorted map, or `null` if it uses the natural ordering (section 20.8) of the keys.

- `Object firstKey()` returns the least key in this sorted map; throws NoSuchElementException if the map is empty.

- `SortedMap headMap(Object to)` returns the sorted map of all entries whose keys are strictly less than `to`. The resulting map is a view of the underlying map.

- `Object lastKey()` returns the greatest key in this sorted map; throws NoSuchElementException if the map is empty.

- `SortedMap subMap(Object from, Object to)` returns the sorted map of all entries whose keys are greater than or equal to `from` and strictly less than `to`. The resulting map is a view of the underlying map.

- `SortedMap tailMap(Object from)` returns the sorted map of all entries whose keys are greater than or equal to `from`. The resulting map is a view of the underlying map.

The TreeMap class implements the SortedMap interface and has the following constructors. The implementation uses balanced ordered binary trees, so all operations are guaranteed to be efficient.

- `TreeMap()` creates an empty map, ordering entries using the `compareTo` method of the keys.

- `TreeMap(Map map)` creates a map containing the entries of `map`, ordering entries using the `compareTo` method of the keys.

- `TreeMap(Comparator cmp)` creates an empty map, ordering entries using `cmp` on the keys.

- `TreeMap(SortedMap s)` creates a map containing the entries of `s`, ordering entries as in `s`.

Example 89 Building a Concordance

This method reads words (alphanumeric tokens) from a text file and creates a concordance, which shows for each word the line numbers of its occurrences. The resulting concordance `index` is a SortedMap from String to SortedSet of `Integer`.

```
static SortedMap buildIndex(String filename) throws IOException {
  Reader r = new BufferedReader(new FileReader(filename));
  StreamTokenizer stok = new StreamTokenizer(r);
  stok.quoteChar('"'); stok.ordinaryChars('!', '/');
  stok.nextToken();
  SortedMap index = new TreeMap();          // Map from String to Set of Integer
  while (stok.ttype != StreamTokenizer.TT_EOF) {
    if (stok.ttype == StreamTokenizer.TT_WORD) {
      SortedSet ts;
      if (index.containsKey(stok.sval))     // If word has a set, get it
        ts = (SortedSet)index.get(stok.sval);
      else {
        ts = new TreeSet();                 // Otherwise create one
        index.put(stok.sval, ts);
      }
      ts.add(new Integer(stok.lineno()));
    }
    stok.nextToken();
  }
  return index;
}
```

Example 90 Storing the Result of a Database Query

This method executes a database query, using classes from the `java.sql` package. It returns the result of the query as an ArrayList with one element for each row in the result. Each row is stored as a HashMap, mapping a result field name to an object (e.g., an Integer or String) holding the value of that field in that row. This is a simple and useful way to separate the database query from the processing of the query result (but it may be too inefficient if the query result is very large).

```
static ArrayList getRows(Connection conn, String query)
  throws SQLException {
  Statement stmt = conn.createStatement();
  ResultSet rset = stmt.executeQuery(query);
  ResultSetMetaData rsmd = rset.getMetaData();
  int columncount = rsmd.getColumnCount();
  ArrayList queryResult = new ArrayList();  // List of Map from String to Object
  while (rset.next()) {
    Map row = new HashMap();
    for (int i=1; i<=columncount; i++)
      row.put(rsmd.getColumnName(i), rset.getObject(i));
    queryResult.add(row);
  }
  return queryResult;
}
```

20.7   Going Through a Collection: Iterator

The Iterator interface provides a standardized way to go through the elements of collections. An Iterator is typically created and used as shown in example 91. The body of the `while` loop should not modify the iterator or the underlying collection; if it does, the result is unpredictable. In fact, the concrete classes ArrayList, LinkedList, HashMap, HashSet, TreeMap, and TreeSet produce fail-fast iterators: if the underlying collection is structurally modified (except by the iterator's `remove` method) after an iterator has been obtained, then a ConcurrentModificationException is thrown. The Iterator interface describes the following methods:

- `boolean hasNext()` returns `true` if a call to `next()` will return a new element.
- `Object next()` returns the next element and advances past that element, if any; throws NoSuchElementException if there is no next element.
- `void remove()` removes the last element returned by the iterator; throws IllegalStateException if no element has been returned by the iterator yet, or if the element has been removed already. Throws UnsupportedOperationException if `remove` is not supported.

An iterator obtained from a List will traverse the elements in the order of the list. An iterator obtained from SortedSet, or from the keys or values of a SortedMap, will traverse the elements in the order of the set elements or the map keys. An iterator obtained from a HashSet will traverse the elements in some unpredictable order. An Iterator provides all the functionality originally provided by the Enumeration interface but has different (shorter) method names.

20.8   Equality, Comparison, and Hash Codes

The elements of a collection must have the `equals` method. If the elements have a `hashCode` method, they can be used as HashSet elements or HashMap keys. If they have the `compareTo` method described by the `java.lang.Comparable` interface, they can be used as TreeSet elements or TreeMap keys. The primitive type wrapper classes (section 5.1) and the String class all have `equals`, `hashCode`, and `compareTo` methods.

- `boolean equals(Object o)` determines the equality of two objects. It is used by ArrayList, LinkedList, HashSet, and HashMap. It should satisfy `o.equals(o)`; if `o1.equals(o2)`, then also `o2.equals(o1)`; and if `o1.equals(o2)` and `o2.equals(o3)`, then also `o1.equals(o3)` for non-null o1, o2, and o3.
- `int hashCode()` returns the hash code of an object. It is used by HashSet and HashMap. It should satisfy that if `o1.equals(o2)`, then `o1.hashCode()==o2.hashCode()`.
- `int compareTo(Object o)`, described by the interface Comparable, performs a three-way comparison of two objects: `o1.compareTo(o2)` is negative if o1 is less than o2, zero if o1 and o2 are equal, and positive if o1 is greater than o2. It is called the *natural ordering* of elements and is used for instance by TreeSet and TreeMap unless a Comparator was given when the set or map was created. It should satisfy that `o1.compareTo(o2)==0` whenever `o1.equals(o2)`.
- `int compare(Object o1, Object o2)`, described by the interface Comparator, performs a three-way comparison of two objects: it is negative if o1 is less than o2, zero if o1 and o2 are equal, and positive if o1 is greater than o2. It can be used to define nonstandard element orderings when creating TreeSets and TreeMaps (example 95). It should satisfy that `compare(o1, o2)==0` whenever `o1.equals(o2)`.

Example 91 Iteration over a Collection

This method prints the elements of the given collection `coll`; it is called in example 88. This is the prototypical way to iterate over a collection. The declaration of `elem` and the type cast immediately inside the `while` loop shows that we expect the collection's elements to have class String.

```
static void traverse(Collection coll) {
  Iterator iter = coll.iterator();
  while (iter.hasNext()) {
    String elem = (String)iter.next();
    System.out.print(elem + " ");
  }
  System.out.println();
}
```

Example 92 Printing a Concordance

The Map index is assumed to be a concordance as created in example 89. The method prints an alphabetical list of the words, and for each word, its line numbers. One iterator is created to go through the words, and for each word, a separate iterator is created to go through the line numbers.

```
static void printIndex(SortedMap index) {
  Iterator wordIter = index.entrySet().iterator();
  while (wordIter.hasNext()) {
    Map.Entry entry = (Map.Entry)wordIter.next();
    System.out.print((String)entry.getKey() + ": ");
    SortedSet lineNoSet = (SortedSet)entry.getValue();
    Iterator lineNoIter = lineNoSet.iterator();
    while (lineNoIter.hasNext())
      System.out.print((Integer)lineNoIter.next() + " ");
    System.out.println();
} }
```

Example 93 A Class Implementing Comparable

A Time object represents the time of day 00:00–23:59. The method call `t1.compareTo(t2)` returns a negative number if `t1` is before `t2`, a positive number if `t1` is after `t2`, and zero if they are the same time. The methods `compareTo`, `equals`, and `hashCode` satisfy the requirements in section 20.8.

```
class Time implements Comparable {
  private int hh, mm;            // 24-hour clock
  public Time(int hh, int mm) { this.hh = hh; this.mm = mm; }

  public int compareTo(Object o) {
    Time t = (Time)o;
    return hh != t.hh ? hh - t.hh : mm - t.mm;
  }

  public boolean equals(Object o) {
    Time t = (Time)o;
    return hh == t.hh && mm == t.mm;
  }

  public int hashCode() { return 60 * hh + mm; }
}
```

20.9   The Utility Class Collections

Class Collections provides static utility methods. The methods `binarySearch`, `max`, `min`, and `sort` also have versions that take an extra Comparator argument and use it to compare elements.

There are static methods similar to `synchronizedList` and `unmodifiableList` for creating a synchronized or unmodifiable view (section 20.1) of a Collection, Set, SortedSet, Map, or SortedMap.

- `static int binarySearch(List lst, Object k)` returns an index `i>=0` for which `lst.get(i)` is equal to k, if any; otherwise returns `i<0` such that `(-i-1)` would be the proper position for k. This is fast for ArrayList but slow for LinkedList. The list `lst` must be sorted, as by `sort(lst)`.

- `static void copy(List dst, List src)` adds all elements from `src` to `dst`, in order.

- `static Enumeration enumeration(Collection coll)` returns an enumeration over `coll`.

- `static void fill(List lst, Object o)` sets all elements of `lst` to o.

- `static Object max(Collection coll)` returns the greatest element of `coll`.
  Throws NoSuchElementException if `coll` is empty.

- `static Object min(Collection coll)` returns the least element of `coll`.
  Throws NoSuchElementException if `coll` is empty.

- `static List nCopies(int n, Object o)` returns an unmodifiable list with n copies of o.

- `static void reverse(List lst)` reverses the order of the elements in `lst`.

- `static Comparator reverseOrder()` returns a comparator that is the reverse of the natural ordering implemented by the `compareTo` method of elements or keys.

- `static void shuffle(List lst)` randomly permutes the elements of `lst`.

- `static boolean replaceAll(List lst, Object o1, Object o2)` replaces all elements equal to o1 by o2 in `lst`; returns `true` if an element was replaced.

- `static void rotate(List lst, int d)` rotates `lst` right by d positions, so `-1` rotates left by one position. Rotates a sublist if applied to a sublist view (section 20.2).

- `static void shuffle(List lst, Random rnd)` randomly permutes the elements of `lst` using `rnd` to generate random numbers.

- `static Set singleton(Object o)` returns an unmodifiable set containing only o.

- `static List singletonList(Object o)` returns an unmodifiable list containing only o.

- `static Map singletonMap(Object k, Object v)` returns an unmodifiable map containing only the entry `(k, v)`.

- `static List synchronizedList(List lst)` returns a synchronized view of `lst`.

- `static void sort(List lst)` sorts `lst` using mergesort and the natural element ordering. This is fast on all Lists.

- `static void swap(List lst, int i, int j)` exchanges the list elements at positions i and j. It throws IndexOutOfBoundsException unless `0 <= i,j` and `i,j < lst.size()`.

- `static List unmodifiableList(List lst)` returns an unmodifiable view of `lst`.

Example 94 Set Membership Test Using HashSet or Binary Search

Imagine that we want to exclude Java reserved names (chapter 2) from the concordance built in example 89, so we need a fast way to recognize such names. Method isKeyword1 uses a HashSet built from a 52-element array of Java keywords, whereas method isKeyword2 uses binary search in the sorted array. The HashSet is two to five times faster in this case.

```
class SetMembership {
  final static String[] keywordarray =
    { "abstract", "assert", "boolean", "break", "byte", ..., "while" };
  final static Set keywords = new HashSet(Arrays.asList(keywordarray));

  static boolean isKeyword1(String id)
  { return keywords.contains(id); }

  static boolean isKeyword2(String id)
  { return Arrays.binarySearch(keywordarray, id) >= 0; }
}
```

Example 95 An Explicit String Comparator

The concordance produced in example 89 uses the built-in compareTo method of String, which orders all upper case letters before all lowercase letters. Thus it would put the string "Create" before "add" before "create". The Comparator class declared here is better because it orders strings so that they appear next to each other if they differ only in case: it would put "add" before "Create" before "create". To use it in example 89, new TreeMap() in that example should be replaced by new TreeMap(new IgnoreCaseComparator()).

```
class IgnoreCaseComparator implements Comparator {
  public int compare(Object o1, Object o2) {
    String s1 = (String)o1, s2 = (String)o2;
    int res = s1.compareToIgnoreCase(s2);
    if (res != 0)
      return res;
    else
      return s1.compareTo(s2);
} }
```

Example 96 Obtaining a Submap

A date book is a sorted map whose keys are Time objects (example 93). We can extract that part of the date book that concerns times on or after 12:00:

```
SortedMap datebook = new TreeMap();    // Map from Time to String
datebook.put(new Time(12, 30), "Lunch");
datebook.put(new Time(15, 30), "Afternoon coffee break");
datebook.put(new Time( 9,  0), "Lecture");
datebook.put(new Time(13, 15), "Board meeting");
SortedMap pm = datebook.tailMap(new Time(12, 0));
Iterator iter = pm.entrySet().iterator();
while (iter.hasNext()) {
  Map.Entry entry = (Map.Entry)iter.next();
  System.out.println((Time)entry.getKey() + " " + (String)entry.getValue());
}
```

20.10   Choosing the Right Collection Class or Map Class

The proper choice of a collection or map class depends on the operations you need to perform on it, and how frequent those operations are. There is no universal best choice.

- LinkedList (section 20.2) or ArrayList (section 20.2 and example 90) should be used for collecting elements for sequential iteration in index order, allowing duplicates.

- HashSet (section 20.3 and example 94) and HashMap (section 20.5 and example 90) are good default choices when random access by element or key is needed, and sequential access in element or key order is not needed. LinkedHashSet and LinkedHashMap additionally guarantee sequential access (using their iterators) in element or key insertion order.

- TreeSet (section 20.4 and example 89) or TreeMap (section 20.6 and example 89) should be used for random access by element or key as well as for iteration in element or key order.

- LinkedList, not ArrayList, should be used for worklist algorithms (example 97), queues, double-ended queues, and stacks.

- ArrayList, not LinkedList, should be used for random access get(i) or set(i, o) by index.

- HashSet or HashMap should be used for sets or maps whose elements or keys are collections, because the collection classes implement useful hashCode methods (example 98).

- For maps whose keys are small nonnegative integers, use ordinary arrays (chapter 8).

The running time or *time complexity* of an operation on a collection is usually given in O notation, as a function of the size n of the collection. Thus $O(1)$ means *constant time*, $O(\log n)$ means *logarithmic time* (time proportional to the logarithm of n), and $O(n)$ means *linear time* (time proportional to n). For accessing, adding, or removing an element, these roughly correspond to *very fast*, *fast*, and *slow*.

In the following table, n is the number of elements in the collection, i is an integer index, and d is the distance from an index i to the nearest end of a list, that is, $\min(i, n-i)$. Thus adding or removing an element of a LinkedList is fast near both ends of the list, where d is small, but for an ArrayList it is fast only near the back end, where $n-i$ is small. The subscript a indicates *amortized complexity*: over a long sequence of operations, the average time per operation is $O(1)$, although any single operation could take time $O(n)$.

Operation	LinkedList	ArrayList	HashSet LinkedHashSet	TreeSet	HashMap LinkedHashMap	TreeMap
add(o) (last)	$O(1)$	$O(1)_a$	$O(1)_a$	$O(\log n)$		
add(i,o)	$O(d)$	$O(n-i)_a$				
addFirst(o)	$O(1)$					
put(k,v)					$O(1)_a$	$O(\log n)$
remove(o)	$O(n)$	$O(n)$	$O(1)$	$O(\log n)$	$O(1)$	$O(\log n)$
remove(i)	$O(d)$	$O(n-i)$				
removeFirst()	$O(1)$					
contains(o)	$O(n)$	$O(n)$	$O(1)$	$O(\log n)$		
containsKey(o)					$O(1)$	$O(\log n)$
containsValue(o)					$O(n)$	$O(n)$
indexOf(o)	$O(n)$	$O(n)$				
get(i)	$O(d)$	$O(1)$				
set(i,o)	$O(d)$	$O(1)$				
get(o)					$O(1)$	$O(\log n)$

Example 97 A Worklist Algorithm

Some algorithms use a so-called *worklist*, containing subproblems still to be solved. For instance, given a set SS of sets of Integers, compute its intersection closure, that is, the least set TT such that SS is a subset of TT and such that for any two sets T_1 and T_2 in TT, their intersection $T_1 \cap T_2$ is also in TT. For instance, if SS is $\{\{2,3\},\{1,3\},\{1,2\}\}$, then TT is $\{\{2,3\},\{1,3\},\{1,2\},\{3\},\{2\},\{1\},\{\}\}$.

The set TT may be computed by putting all elements of SS in a worklist, then repeatedly selecting an element S from the worklist, adding it to TT, and for every set T already in TT, adding the intersection of S and T to the worklist if not already in TT. When the worklist is empty, TT is intersection-closed.

The epsilon closure of a state of a nondeterministic finite automaton (NFA) may be computed using the same approach; see the full program text underlying example 98.

```
static Set intersectionClose(Set SS) {
  LinkedList worklist = new LinkedList(SS);
  Set TT = new HashSet();
  while (!worklist.isEmpty()) {
    Set S = (Set)worklist.removeLast();
    Iterator TTIter = TT.iterator();
    while (TTIter.hasNext()) {
      Set TS = new TreeSet((Set)TTIter.next());
      TS.retainAll(S);        // Intersection of T and S
      if (!TT.contains(TS))
        worklist.add(TS);
    }
    TT.add(S);
  }
  return TT;
}
```

Example 98 Using Sets as Keys in a HashMap

The standard algorithm for turning a nondeterministic finite automaton (NFA) into a deterministic finite automaton (DFA) creates composite automaton states that are sets of integers. It is preferable to replace such composite states by simple integers. This method takes as argument a collection of composite states and returns a renamer, which is a map from composite state names (Sets of Integers) to simple state names (Integers).

```
static Map mkRenamer(Collection states) {
  Map renamer = new HashMap();
  Iterator iter = states.iterator();
  while (iter.hasNext()) {
    Set k = (Set)iter.next();
    renamer.put(k, new Integer(renamer.size()));
  }
  return renamer;
}
```

21   Input and Output

Sequential input and output uses objects called *streams*. There are two kinds of streams: *character streams* and *byte streams*, also called text streams and binary streams. Character streams are used for input from text files and human-readable output to text files, printers, and so on, using 16-bit Unicode characters. Byte streams are used for compact and efficient input and output of primitive data (int, double, ...) as well as objects and arrays, in machine-readable form.

There are separate classes for handling character streams and byte streams. The classes for character input and output are called Readers and Writers. The classes for byte input and output are called InputStreams and OutputStreams. This chapter describes input and output using the java.io package. Java 2, version 1.4, provides additional facilities in package java.nio, not described here.

One can create subclasses of the stream classes, overriding inherited methods to obtain specialized stream classes. We shall not further discuss how to do that here.

The four stream class hierarchies are shown in the following table, with related input and output classes shown on the same line. The table shows, for instance, that BufferedReader and FilterReader are subclasses of Reader, and that LineNumberReader is a subclass of BufferedReader. Abstract classes are shown in *italics*.

	Input Streams	Output Streams
Character Streams	*Reader*	*Writer*
	BufferedReader	BufferedWriter
	LineNumberReader	
	FilterReader	*FilterWriter*
	PushBackReader	
	InputStreamReader	OutputStreamWriter
	FileReader	FileWriter
	PipedReader	PipedWriter
		PrintWriter
	CharArrayReader	CharArrayWriter
	StringReader	StringWriter
Byte Streams	*InputStream*	*OutputStream*
	ByteArrayInputStream	ByteArrayOutputStream
	FileInputStream	FileOutputStream
	FilterInputStream	FilterOutputStream
	BufferedInputStream	BufferedOutputStream
	DataInputStream	DataOutputStream
	PushBackInputStream	
		PrintStream
	ObjectInputStream	ObjectOutputStream
	PipedInputStream	PipedOutputStream
	SequenceInputStream	
	RandomAccessFile	

The classes DataInputStream, ObjectInputStream, and RandomAccessFile implement the interface DataInput, and the classes DataOutputStream, ObjectOutputStream and RandomAccessFile implement the interface DataOutput (section 21.10).

The class ObjectInputStream implements interface ObjectInput, and class ObjectOutputStream implements interface ObjectOutput (section 21.11).

21.1 Creating Streams from Other Streams

A stream may either be created outright (e.g., a FileInputStream may be created and associated with a named file on disk, for reading from that file) or it may be created from an existing stream to provide additional features (e.g., a BufferedInputStream may be created in terms of a FileInputStream, for more efficient input). In any case, an input stream or reader has an underlying source of data to read from, and an output stream or writer has an underlying sink of data to write to. The following figure shows how streams may be defined in terms of existing streams, or in terms of other data.

The stream classes are divided along two lines: character streams (top) versus byte streams (bottom), and input streams (left) versus output streams (right). The arrows show what streams can be created from other streams. For instance, the arrow from InputStream to InputStreamReader shows that one can create an InputStreamReader from an InputStream. The arrow from Reader to BufferedReader shows that one can create a BufferedReader from a Reader. Since an InputStreamReader is a Reader, one can create a BufferedReader from an existing InputStream (such as `System.in`) in two steps, as shown in example 99. On the other hand, there is no way to create a PipedOutputStream from a File or a file name; a PipedOutputStream must be created outright, or from an existing PipedInputStream, and similarly for other pipes (section 21.15).

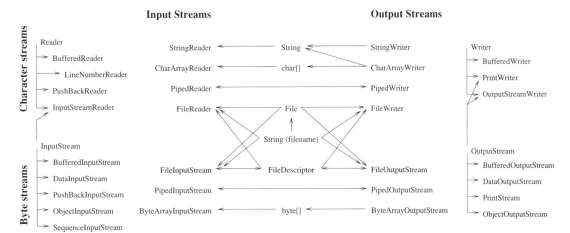

Example 99 A Complete Input-Output Example

```java
import java.io.*;
class BasicIOExample {
  public static void main(String[] args) throws IOException {
    BufferedReader r = new BufferedReader(new InputStreamReader(System.in));
    int count = 0;
    String s = r.readLine();
    while (s != null && !s.equals("")) {
      count++;
      s = r.readLine();
    }
    System.out.println("You entered " + count + " nonempty lines");
} }
```

21.2   Kinds of Input and Output Methods

The following table summarizes the naming conventions for methods of the input and output classes as well as their main characteristics, such as their end-of-stream behavior.

Method Name	Effect
read	Inputs characters from a Reader (section 21.4) or inputs bytes from an InputStream (section 21.8). It *blocks*, that is, does not return, until some input is available; returns -1 on end-of-stream.
write	Outputs characters to a Writer (section 21.5) or outputs bytes to an OutputStream (section 21.9).
print	Converts a value (int, double, ..., object) to textual representation and outputs it to a PrintWriter or PrintStream (section 21.6).
println	Same as print but outputs a newline after printing.
read*t*	Inputs a value of primitive type *t* from a DataInput stream (section 21.10). Blocks until some input is available; throws EOFException on end-of-stream.
write*t*	Outputs a primitive value of primitive type *t* to a DataOutput stream (section 21.10).
readObject	Deserializes objects from an ObjectInput stream (section 21.11). Blocks until some input is available; throws ObjectStreamException on end-of-stream.
writeObject	Serializes objects to an ObjectOutput stream (section 21.11).
skip(n)	Skips at most n bytes (from InputStreams) or n characters (from Readers). If n>0, blocks until some input is available; if n<0, throws IllegalArgumentException; returns 0 on end-of-stream.
flush	Writes any buffered data to the underlying stream, then flushes that stream. The effect is to make sure that all data have actually been written to the file system or the network.
close	Flushes and closes the stream, then flushes and closes all underlying streams. Further operations on the stream, except close, will throw IOException. Buffered writers and output streams should be explicitly closed or flushed to make sure that all data have been written; otherwise output may be lost, even in case of normal program termination.

21.3   Imports, Exceptions, Thread Safety

A program using the input and output classes must contain the import declaration

```
import java.io.*;
```

Most input and output operations can throw an exception of class IOException or one of its subclasses, all of which are checked exceptions (chapter 14). Hence a method doing input or output must either do so in a try-catch block (section 12.6.6) or must contain the declaration throws IOException (section 9.8).

The standard implementation of input-output is thread-safe: multiple concurrent threads (chapter 15) can safely read from or write to the same stream without corrupting it. However, the Java class library documentation is not explicit on this point, so probably one should avoid using the same stream from multiple threads, or explicitly synchronize on the stream.

Example 100 Input-Output: Twelve Examples in One
This example illustrates input and output with human-readable text files; input and output of primitive values
with binary files; input and output of arrays and objects with binary files; input and output of primitive values
with random access binary files; input and output using strings and string buffers; output to standard output
and standard error; and input from standard input.

  Although these brief examples do not use buffering, input and output from files, sockets, and so on, should
use buffering for efficiency (section 21.12).

```java
// Write numbers and words on file "f.txt" in human-readable form:
PrintWriter pwr = new PrintWriter(new FileWriter("f.txt"));
pwr.print(4711); pwr.print(' '); pwr.print("cool"); pwr.close();
// Read numbers and words from human-readable text file "f.txt":
StreamTokenizer stok = new StreamTokenizer(new FileReader("f.txt"));
int tok = stok.nextToken();
while (tok != StreamTokenizer.TT_EOF)
  { System.out.println(stok.sval); tok = stok.nextToken(); }
// Write primitive values to a binary file "p.dat":
DataOutputStream dos = new DataOutputStream(new FileOutputStream("p.dat"));
dos.writeInt(4711); dos.writeChar(' '); dos.writeUTF("cool"); dos.close();
// Read primitive values from binary file "p.dat":
DataInputStream dis = new DataInputStream(new FileInputStream("p.dat"));
System.out.println(dis.readInt()+"|"+dis.readChar()+"|"+ dis.readUTF());
// Write an object or array to binary file "o.dat":
ObjectOutputStream oos = new ObjectOutputStream(new FileOutputStream("o.dat"));
oos.writeObject(new int[] { 2, 3, 5, 7, 11 }); oos.close();
// Read objects or arrays from binary file "o.dat":
ObjectInputStream ois = new ObjectInputStream(new FileInputStream("o.dat"));
int[] ia = (int[])(ois.readObject());
System.out.println(ia[0]+","+ia[1]+","+ia[2]+","+ia[3]+","+ia[4]);
// Read and write parts of file "raf.dat" in arbitrary order:
RandomAccessFile raf = new RandomAccessFile("raf.dat", "rw");
raf.writeDouble(3.1415); raf.writeInt(42);
raf.seek(0); System.out.println(raf.readDouble() + " " + raf.readInt());
// Read from a String s as if it were a text file:
Reader r = new StringReader("abc");
System.out.println("abc: " + (char)r.read() + (char)r.read() + (char)r.read());
// Write to a StringBuffer as if it were a text file:
Writer sw = new StringWriter();
sw.write('d'); sw.write('e'); sw.write('f');
System.out.println(sw.toString());
// Write characters to standard output and standard error:
System.out.println("std output"); System.err.println("std error");
// Read characters from standard input (the keyboard):
System.out.print("Type some characters and press Enter: ");
BufferedReader bisr = new BufferedReader(new InputStreamReader(System.in));
String response = bisr.readLine();
System.out.println("You typed: '" + response + "'");
// Read a byte from standard input (the keyboard):
System.out.print("Type one character and press Enter: ");
byte b = (byte)System.in.read();
System.out.println("First byte of your input is: " + b);
```

21.4 Sequential Character Input: Readers

The abstract class Reader and its subclasses (all having names ending in Reader) are used for character-oriented sequential input. In addition to the classes shown here, see BufferedReader (section 21.12) and LineNumber-Reader (example 105). The Reader class has the following methods:

- void close() flushes and closes the stream and any underlying stream. Any subsequent operation, except close, will throw IOException.
- void mark(int limt) marks the current input position, permitting at least limt characters to be read before calling reset.
- boolean markSupported() is true if the reader supports setting of marks and resetting to latest mark.
- int read() reads one character (with code 0...65535) and returns it. Blocks until input is available, or end-of-stream is reached (and then returns −1), or an error occurs (and then throws IOException).
- int read(char[] b) reads at most b.length characters into b and returns the number of characters read. Returns immediately if b.length is 0, else blocks until at least one character is available; returns −1 on end-of-stream.
- int read(char[] b, int i, int n) works like the preceding, but reads into buf[i..(i+n-1)]. Throws IndexOutOfBoundsException if i<0 or n<0 or i+n>b.length.
- boolean ready() returns true if the next read or skip will not block.
- void reset() resets the stream to the position of the latest call to mark.
- int skip(int n) skips at most n characters and returns the number of characters skipped; returns 0 on end-of-stream.

21.4.1 Reading Characters from a Byte Stream: InputStreamReader

An InputStreamReader is a reader (a character input stream) that reads from a byte input stream, assembling bytes into characters using a character encoding. It performs buffered input from the underlying stream. An InputStreamReader has the same methods as a Reader (section 21.4), and also this constructor and method:

- InputStreamReader(InputStream is) creates a character input stream (a reader) from byte input stream is, using the platform's standard character encoding.
- String getEncoding() returns the canonical name of the character encoding used by this InputStream-Reader, for instance, "ISO8859_1" or "Cp1252".

21.4.2 Sequential Character Input from a File: FileReader

A FileReader is a buffered character input stream associated with a (sequential) file, and equivalent to an InputStreamReader created from a FileInputStream. It has the same methods as InputStreamReader, and these constructors:

- FileReader(String name) creates a character input stream associated with the named file on the file system. Throws FileNotFoundException if the named file does not exist, is a directory, or cannot be opened for some other reason.
- FileReader(File file) creates a character input stream from the given file in the file system.
- FileReader(FileDescriptor fd) creates a character input stream from the file descriptor.

21.5 Sequential Character Output: Writers

The abstract class Writer and its subclasses (all having names ending in Writer) are used for character-oriented sequential output. They have the following methods:

- `void close()` flushes and closes the stream.
- `void flush()` actually writes data to the underlying stream or file, and then flushes that.
- `void write(char[] b)` writes the contents of character array b.
- `void write(char[] b, int i, int n)` writes n characters from b starting at position i; throws IndexOutOfBoundsException if i<0 or n<0 or i+n>b.length.
- `void write(int c)` writes a single character, namely, the two low-order bytes of c.
- `void write(String s)` writes string s.
- `void write(String s, int i, int n)` writes n characters from s starting at position i; throws StringIndexOutOfBoundsException if i<0 or n<0 or i+n>s.length.

21.5.1 Writing Characters to a Byte Stream: OutputStreamWriter

An OutputStreamWriter is a writer (character output stream) that writes to a byte output stream, converting characters to bytes using a character encoding. It performs buffered output to the underlying stream. An OutputStreamWriter has the same methods as a Writer (section 21.5), and in addition these constructors and method:

- `OutputStreamWriter(OutputStream os)` creates an OutputStreamWriter that writes to stream os using the platform's default character encoding.
- `OutputStreamWriter(OutputStream os, String enc)` creates an OutputStreamWriter that writes to stream os using the character encoding specified by enc.
- `String getEncoding()` returns the canonical name of the character encoding used by this OutputStreamWriter, for instance, `"ISO8859_1"` or `"Cp1252"`.

21.5.2 Sequential Character Output to a File: FileWriter

A FileWriter is a buffered character output stream associated with a (sequential) file, equivalent to an OutputStreamWriter created from a FileOutputStream. It has the same methods as OutputStreamWriter, and these constructors:

- `FileWriter(String name)` creates a character output stream and associates it with the named file in the file system. If the file exists, then it truncates the file; otherwise it tries to create a new empty file. Throws FileNotFoundException if the named file is a directory or cannot be opened or created for some other reason.
- `FileWriter(String file, boolean append)` works like the previous method, but if append is true, it does not truncate the file: instead output will be appended to the existing file contents.
- `FileWriter(File file)` works like the previous method, but creates the writer from file.
- `FileWriter(FileDescriptor fd)` works like the previous method, but creates the writer from fd.

21.6 Printing Primitive Data to a Character Stream: PrintWriter

The class PrintWriter is used to output primitive data to text files in human-readable form. Unlike the methods of other Writers, those of PrintWriter never throw IOException but set the error status. The PrintWriter class has all the methods of Writer, and in addition these constructors and methods:

- `PrintWriter(OutputStream os)` creates a PrintWriter that prints to stream `os`, without autoflush.
- `PrintWriter(OutputStream os, boolean flush)` creates a PrintWriter that prints to output stream `os`; if `flush` is `true`, then it flushes the writer after every call to `println`.
- `PrintWriter(Writer wr)` creates a PrintWriter that prints to the writer `wr`, without autoflush.
- `PrintWriter(Writer wr, boolean flush)` creates a PrintWriter that prints to the writer `wr`; if `flush` is `true`, then it flushes the writer after every call to `println`.
- `boolean checkError()` flushes the stream, then returns `true` if an error has ever occurred.
- `void print(boolean b)` prints the boolean `b`, that is, `true` or `false`.
- `void print(char c)` prints the character `c`.
- `void print(char[] s)` prints the characters in `s`.
- `void print(double d)` prints the double `d`.
- `void print(float f)` prints the float `f`.
- `void print(int i)` prints the integer `i`.
- `void print(long l)` prints the long integer `l`.
- `void print(Object obj)` prints the object using `obj.toString()`.
- `void print(String s)` prints the string `s`.
- `void println()` prints a single newline.
- `void println(e)` works like `print(e)` followed by `println()`.

21.6.1 Standard Output: `System.out` and `System.err` Are PrintStreams

The standard output stream `System.out` and standard error stream `System.err` are PrintStreams. PrintStream is a subclass of OutputStream but in addition has methods `print` and `println` for character-based output, just as PrintWriter. These methods convert characters to bytes using the default encoding; to use another encoding enc, write instead to a PrintWriter created by `new PrintWriter(new OutputStreamWriter(System.out), enc)`. The methods of a PrintStream never throw IOException, but set the error status; use `checkError()` to test the error status.

21.6.2 Formatting Numbers for Character Output: DecimalFormat

Proper layout of text printed with PrintWriter requires detailed formatting control. The formatting of numbers can be controlled using the class DecimalFormat from the `java.text` package. The table on the facing page shows some DecimalFormat patterns and their effects.

There are many other facilities for formatting text output in the package `java.text`. Unlike languages such as C, C#, Fortran, and Pascal, Java has no standard mechanism for aligning numbers and words in columns. Such mechanisms produce the desired result only with fixed-pitch fonts. A simple method for padding a string on the left (for right alignment) is shown in example 103.

Example 101 Printing Numbers to a Text File
Simulate 1,000 rolls of a die and print the outcome to the text file `dice.txt`, 20 numbers to a line:

```
PrintWriter pw = new PrintWriter(new FileWriter("dice.txt"));
for (int i=1; i<=1000; i++) {
  int die = (int)(1 + 6 * Math.random());
  pw.print(die); pw.print(' ');
  if (i % 20 == 0) pw.println();
}
pw.println();
pw.close();                 // Without this, the output file may be empty
```

Example 102 Printing an HTML Table
This example generates a temperature conversion table in HTML. The Fahrenheit temperature f corresponds to the Celsius temperature $c = 5 \cdot (f - 32)/9$. The number of fractional digits is controlled by a DecimalFormat object. The HTML TABLE tag is used to control the alignment of numbers into columns.

```
PrintWriter pw = new PrintWriter(new FileWriter("temperature.html"));
DecimalFormat ff = new DecimalFormat("#0"), cf = new DecimalFormat("0.0");
pw.println("<TABLE BORDER><TR><TH>Fahrenheit<TH>Celsius</TR>");
for (double f=100; f<=400; f+=10) {
  double c = 5 * (f - 32) / 9;
  pw.println("<TR ALIGN=RIGHT><TD>" + ff.format(f) + "<TD>" + cf.format(c));
}
pw.println("</TABLE>");
pw.close();                 // Without this, the output file may be empty
```

Example 103 Printing a Text Table
To print a conversion table in text format in a fixed-pitch font, replace the second `pw.println` call in example 102 by `pw.println(padLeft(ff.format(f), 10) + padLeft(cf.format(c), 10))`, which uses the method `padLeft` from example 87 to align numbers to the right.

Some DecimalFormat Patterns and Their Effect

Number	DecimalFormat Pattern							
	#	#.#	#.##	0.0	0.0#	0.00	000.0	#,##0.00
0.0	0	0	0	0.0	0.0	0.00	000.0	0.00
0.1	0	0.1	0.1	0.1	0.1	0.10	000.1	0.10
1.0	1	1	1	1.0	1.0	1.00	001.0	1.00
1.5	2	1.5	1.5	1.5	1.5	1.50	001.5	1.50
2.5	2	2.5	2.5	2.5	2.5	2.50	002.5	2.50
−1.5	-2	-1.5	-1.5	-1.5	-1.5	-1.50	-001.5	-1.50
330.8	331	330.8	330.8	330.8	330.8	330.80	330.8	330.80
1234.516	1235	1234.5	1234.52	1234.5	1234.52	1234.52	1234.5	1,234.52

21.7   Reading Primitive Data from a Character Stream: StreamTokenizer

Reading words and numbers from a character stream is more complicated than printing them, so there is no text input counterpart to PrintWriter. Instead create a StreamTokenizer from a Reader.

A StreamTokenizer collects characters into tokens. Characters are classified as white space (separating tokens), number characters (making up a number token), word characters (making up a word token), quote characters (delimiting a string token), end-line comment characters (initiating a comment extending to end-of-line), or ordinary characters (none of the preceding).

A StreamTokenizer can be created and configured using this constructor and these methods and fields:

- `StreamTokenizer(Reader r)` creates a StreamTokenizer that reads from stream `r`.
- `void commentChar(int ch)` tells the tokenizer that `ch` is an end-line comment character.
- `void eolIsSignificant(boolean b)` tells the tokenizer to consider newline as a separate token of type `TT_EOL`, not as white space, if `b` is `true`.
- `void ordinaryChars(int c1, int c2)` tells the tokenizer that any character in the range `c1..c2` (inclusive) is an ordinary character: a single-character token, with `ttype` set to the character code.
- `void parseNumbers()` tells the tokenizer to recognize number tokens. A number token is a "word" beginning with a decimal digit (`0..9`) or a decimal point (`.`) or a minus sign (`-`), and consisting only of these three kinds of characters, so numbers in scientific notation `6.02e23` are not recognized. A number token has type `TT_NUMBER`.
- `void quoteChar(int ch)` tells the tokenizer that character `ch` is a string delimiter. When this character is encountered, `ttype` is set to `ch`, and `sval` is set to the string's contents: the characters strictly between `ch` and the next occurrence of `ch` or newline or end-of-stream.
- `void resetSyntax()` makes all characters ordinary; see `ordinaryChars`.
- `void whitespaceChars(int c1, int c2)` tells the tokenizer that all characters in the range `c1..c2` (inclusive) are white space also, that is, token separators.
- `void wordChars(int c1, int c2)` tells the tokenizer that all characters in the range `c1..c2` (inclusive) are word characters also.

Class StreamTokenizer has these methods and fields for reading values:

- `int lineno()` returns the current line number, counting from 1.
- `int nextToken()` reads the next (or first) token and returns its type.
- `double nval` is the number value of the current number token (when `ttype` is `TT_NUMBER`).
- `String sval` is the string value of the current word token (when `ttype` is `TT_WORD`), or the string body of the current string token (when `ttype` is a quote character).
- `int ttype` is the type of the current token. The type may be `StreamTokenizer.TT_NUMBER`, indicating a number, or `StreamTokenizer.TT_WORD`, indicating a word, or `StreamTokenizer.TT_EOL`, indicating a newline, or `StreamTokenizer.TT_EOF`, indicating end-of-stream (no more tokens), or a quote character, indicating a string (in quotes), or any other character, indicating that character as a token by itself.

While a StreamTokenizer is useful for reading fairly simple text files, more structured text files should be read using a proper lexer and parser (see common textbooks for compiler courses) or special-purpose libraries (e.g., for XML files or XML streams).

Example 104 Reading Numbers from a Text File
A StreamTokenizer stok is created from a buffered file reader and told to recognize number tokens. Tokens are read until end-of-stream, and the number tokens are added together, whereas nonnumber tokens are printed to standard output. The buffering is important: it makes the program more than 20 times faster.

```
static void sumfile(String filename) throws IOException {
  Reader r = new BufferedReader(new FileReader(filename));
  StreamTokenizer stok = new StreamTokenizer(r);
  stok.parseNumbers();
  double sum = 0;
  stok.nextToken();
  while (stok.ttype != StreamTokenizer.TT_EOF) {
    if (stok.ttype == StreamTokenizer.TT_NUMBER)
      sum += stok.nval;
    else
      System.out.println("Nonnumber: " + stok.sval);
    stok.nextToken();
  }
  System.out.println("The file sum is " + sum);
}
```

Example 105 Reading Numbers from a Text File, Line by Line
A StreamTokenizer stok is created from a LineNumberReader and told to recognize number tokens and new-lines. Tokens are read until end-of-stream, and the sum of the number tokens is computed line by line. The line number is set to count from 1 (default is 0). Class LineNumberReader is a subclass of BufferedReader and therefore is already buffered. Using a LineNumberReader is somewhat redundant, since StreamTokenizer itself provides a lineno() method.

```
static void sumlines(String filename) throws IOException {
  LineNumberReader lnr = new LineNumberReader(new FileReader(filename));
  lnr.setLineNumber(1);
  StreamTokenizer stok = new StreamTokenizer(lnr);
  stok.parseNumbers();
  stok.eolIsSignificant(true);
  stok.nextToken();
  while (stok.ttype != StreamTokenizer.TT_EOF) {
    int lineno = lnr.getLineNumber();
    double sum = 0;
    while (stok.ttype != StreamTokenizer.TT_EOL) {
      if (stok.ttype == StreamTokenizer.TT_NUMBER)
        sum += stok.nval;
      stok.nextToken();
    }
    System.out.println("Sum of line " + lineno + " is " + sum);
    stok.nextToken();
  }
}
```

21.8 Sequential Byte Input: InputStream

The abstract class InputStream and its subclasses (all of whose names end in InputStream) are used for byte-oriented sequential input. They have the following methods:

- `int available()` returns the number of bytes that can be read or skipped without blocking.
- `void close()` closes the stream.
- `void mark(int limt)` marks the current input position, permitting at least `limt` bytes to be read before calling `reset`.
- `boolean markSupported()` returns `true` if the stream supports `mark` and `reset`.
- `int read()` reads one byte $(0 \ldots 255)$ and returns it, blocking until input is available; returns -1 on end-of-stream.
- `int read(byte[] b)` reads at most `b.length` bytes into b, blocking until at least one byte is available; then returns the number of bytes actually read. Returns -1 on end-of-stream.
- `int read(byte[] b, int i, int n)` reads at most n bytes into b at position i, blocking until at least one byte is available, and returns the number of bytes actually read. Returns -1 on end-of-stream. Throws IndexOutOfBoundsException if `i<0` or `n<0` or `i+n>b.length`.
- `void reset()` repositions the stream to the position at which the `mark` method was last called.
- `long skip(long n)` skips at most n bytes, blocking until a byte is available, and returns the number of bytes actually skipped. Returns 0 if end-of-stream is reached before input is available.

The standard input `System.in` is an InputStream; to read characters from it, create an InputStreamReader using `new InputStreamReader(System.in)`; see example 100.

21.8.1 Sequential Byte Input from File: FileInputStream

A FileInputStream is an InputStream that reads sequentially from an existing file on the file system. It has the same methods as InputStream (section 21.8), and these constructors and additional method:

- `FileInputStream(String name)` creates a byte input stream and associates it with file `name` in the file system. Throws FileNotFoundException if the file does not exist, is a directory, or cannot be opened.
- `FileInputStream(File file)` works like the preceding, but associates the stream with `file`.
- `FileInputStream(FileDescriptor fd)` works like the preceding, but associates the stream with `fd`.
- `FileDescriptor getFD()` returns the file descriptor associated with this stream.

21.8.2 Sequential Binary Input of Primitive Data: DataInputStream

Class DataInputStream provides methods for machine-independent sequential binary input of Java primitive types such as `int` and `double`. The class implements the DataInput interface (section 21.10) and in addition provides this constructor and static method:

- `DataInputStream(InputStream is)` creates a DataInputStream that reads from stream `is`.
- `static String readUTF(DataInput di)` reads a Java UTF-8 encoded string from stream `di`.

Class DataInputStream also has a `readLine` method, which is deprecated. To read lines of text from a DataInputStream, create an InputStreamReader (section 21.4.1) from it instead.

21.9   Sequential Byte Output: OutputStream

The abstract class OutputStream and its subclasses (all of whose names end in OutputStream) are used for byte-oriented sequential output. It has the following methods:

- void close() closes the output stream.
- void flush() flushes the output stream and forces any buffered output bytes to be written to the underlying stream or file, then flushes that.
- void write(byte[] b) writes b.length bytes from b to the output stream.
- void write(byte[] b, int i, int n) writes n bytes from b starting at offset i to the output stream. Throws IndexOutOfBoundsException if i<0 or n<0 or i+n>b.length.
- void write(int b) writes the byte b (0...255) to the output stream.

21.9.1   Sequential Byte Output to a File: FileOutputStream

A FileOutputStream is an OutputStream that writes sequentially to a file on the file system. It has the same methods as OutputStream (section 21.9) and these constructors and additional method:

- FileOutputStream(String name) creates a byte output stream and associates it with the named file in the file system. If the file exists, then it truncates the file; otherwise, it attempts to create the file. Throws FileNotFoundException if the file is a directory or cannot be opened or created for some other reason.
- FileOutputStream(String name, boolean append) works like the preceding, but if append is true, then does not truncate the file: instead output will be appended to the existing file contents.
- FileOutputStream(File file) works like the preceding, but associates the stream with file.
- FileOutputStream(FileDescriptor fd) works like the preceding, but associates the stream with fd.
- FileDescriptor getFD() returns the file descriptor associated with this stream.

21.9.2   Sequential Binary Output of Primitive Data: DataOutputStream

Class DataOutputStream provides methods for machine-independent sequential binary output of Java primitive types such as int and double. The class implements the DataOutput interface (section 21.10) and provides this constructor and method:

- DataOutputStream(OutputStream os) creates an DataOutputStream that writes to the stream os.
- int size() returns the number of bytes written to this DataOutputStream.

21.10   Binary Input-Output of Primitive Data: DataInput and DataOutput

The interfaces DataInput and DataOutput describe operations for byte-oriented input and output of values of primitive type, such as `boolean`, `int`, and `double`. Thus DataInput's method `readInt()` is suitable for reading integers written using DataOutput's method `writeInt(int)`. The data format is platform-independent.

The DataInput interface describes the following methods. The `read` and `skip` methods block until the required number of bytes have become available, and throw EOFException if end-of-stream is reached first.

- `boolean readBoolean()` reads one input byte and returns `true` if nonzero, `false` otherwise.
- `byte readByte()` reads one input byte and returns a byte in range $-128\ldots127$.
- `char readChar()` reads two bytes and returns a character in range $0\ldots65535$.
- `double readDouble()` reads eight bytes and returns a double.
- `float readFloat()` reads four bytes and returns a float.
- `void readFully(byte[] b)` reads exactly `b.length` bytes into buffer `b`.
- `void readFully(byte[] b, int i, int n)` reads exactly n bytes into `b[i..(i+n-1)]`.
- `int readInt()` reads four bytes and returns an integer.
- `String readLine()` reads a line of one-byte characters in the range $0\ldots255$ (not Unicode).
- `long readLong()` reads eight bytes and returns a long integer.
- `short readShort()` reads two bytes and returns a short integer $-32768\ldots32676$.
- `int readUnsignedByte()` reads one byte and returns an integer in the range $0\ldots255$.
- `int readUnsignedShort()` reads two bytes and returns an integer in the range $0\ldots65535$.
- `String readUTF()` reads a string encoded using the Java modified UTF-8 format.
- `int skipBytes(int n)` skips exactly n bytes of data and returns n.

The DataOutput interface describes the following methods. Note that `writeInt(i)` writes four bytes representing the Java integer `i`, whereas `write(i)` writes one byte containing the low-order eight bits of `i`.

- `void write(byte[] b)` writes all the bytes from array `b`.
- `void write(byte[] b, int i, int n)` writes n bytes from array `b[i..(i+n-1)]`.
- `void write(int v)` writes the eight low-order bits of byte `v`.
- `void writeBoolean(boolean v)` writes one byte: 1 if `v` is `true`, otherwise 0.
- `void writeByte(int v)` writes the low-order byte (eight low-order bits) of integer `v`.
- `void writeBytes(String s)` writes the low-order byte of each character in `s` (not Unicode).
- `void writeChar(int v)` writes two bytes (high-order, low-order) representing `v`.
- `void writeChars(String s)` writes the string `s`, two bytes per character.
- `void writeDouble(double v)` writes eight bytes representing `v`.
- `void writeFloat(float v)` writes four bytes representing `v`.
- `void writeInt(int v)` writes four bytes representing `v`.
- `void writeLong(long v)` writes eight bytes representing `v`.
- `void writeShort(int v)` writes two bytes representing `v`.
- `void writeUTF(String s)` writes two bytes of (byte) length information, followed by the Java modified UTF-8 representation of every character in the string `s`.

Example 106 Binary Input and Output of Primitive Data

Method `writedata` demonstrates all ways to write primitive data to a DataOutput stream (a stream of class DataInputStream or RandomAccessFile). Similarly, method `readdata` demonstrates all ways to read primitive values from a DataInput stream (a stream of class DataOutputStream or RandomAccessFile). The methods complement each other, so after writing a stream with `writedata`, one can read it using `readdata`.

```
public static void main(String[] args) throws IOException {
  DataOutputStream daos = new DataOutputStream(new FileOutputStream("tmp1.dat"));
  writedata(daos); daos.close();
  DataInputStream dais = new DataInputStream(new FileInputStream("tmp1.dat"));
  readdata(dais);
  RandomAccessFile raf = new RandomAccessFile("tmp2.dat", "rw");
  writedata(raf); raf.seek(0); readdata(raf);
}
static void writedata(DataOutput out) throws IOException {
  out.writeBoolean(true);                       // Write 1 byte
  out.writeByte(120);                           // Write 1 byte
  out.writeBytes("foo");                        // Write 3 bytes
  out.writeBytes("fo");                         // Write 2 bytes
  out.writeChar('A');                           // Write 2 bytes
  out.writeChars("foo");                        // Write 6 bytes
  out.writeDouble(300.1);                       // Write 8 bytes
  out.writeFloat(300.2F);                       // Write 4 bytes
  out.writeInt(1234);                           // Write 4 bytes
  out.writeLong(12345L);                        // Write 8 bytes
  out.writeShort(32000);                        // Write 2 bytes
  out.writeUTF("foo");                          // Write 2 + 3 bytes
  out.writeUTF("Rhône");                        // Write 2 + 6 bytes
  out.writeByte(-1);                            // Write 1 byte
  out.writeShort(-1);                           // Write 2 bytes
}
static void readdata(DataInput in) throws IOException {
  byte[] buf1 = new byte[3];
  System.out.print(       in.readBoolean());          // Read 1 byte
  System.out.print(" " + in.readByte());              // Read 1 byte
  in.readFully(buf1);                                  // Read 3 bytes
  in.readFully(buf1, 0, 2);                            // Read 2 bytes
  System.out.print(" " + in.readChar());              // Read 2 bytes
  System.out.print(" " + in.readChar()+in.readChar()+in.readChar());
  System.out.print(" " + in.readDouble());            // Read 8 bytes
  System.out.print(" " + in.readFloat());             // Read 4 bytes
  System.out.print(" " + in.readInt());               // Read 4 bytes
  System.out.print(" " + in.readLong());              // Read 8 bytes
  System.out.print(" " + in.readShort());             // Read 2 bytes
  System.out.print(" " + in.readUTF());               // Read 2 + 3 bytes
  System.out.print(" " + in.readUTF());               // Read 2 + 6 bytes
  System.out.print(" " + in.readUnsignedByte());      // Read 1 byte
  System.out.print(" " + in.readUnsignedShort());     // Read 2 bytes
  System.out.println();
}
```

21.11   Serialization of Objects: ObjectInput and ObjectOutput

The interfaces ObjectInput and ObjectOutput describe operations for byte-oriented input and output of values of reference type, that is, objects and arrays. This is also called *serialization*.

An object or array can be serialized (converted to a sequence of bytes) if its class and all classes on which the object or array depends have been declared to implement the interface Serializable. The Serializable interface does not declare any methods; it only serves to show that the class admits serialization.

Serialization of an object o writes the object's nonstatic (instance) fields, except those declared transient, to the stream. When the object is deserialized, a transient field gets the default value for its type (false or 0 or 0.0 or null). Class fields (static fields) are not serialized.

Serialization to an ObjectOutputStream preserves sharing among the objects written to it, and more generally, preserves the form of the object reference graph. For instance, if object o1 and o2 both refer to a common object c (so o1.c == o2.c), and o1 and o2 are serialized to ObjectOutputStream oos, then object c is serialized only once to oos. When o1 and o2 are restored again from oos, then c is restored also, exactly once, so o1.c == o2.c holds as before. If o1 and o2 are serialized to two different ObjectOutputStreams, then restoration of o1 and o2 will produce two distinct copies of c, so o1.c != o2.c. Thus sharing among objects is not preserved across multiple ObjectOutputStreams.

The interface ObjectInput has all the methods specified by DataInput, and the following additional ones. Class ObjectInputStream implements ObjectInput. The methods available(), close(), read(byte[]), read(byte[], int, int), and skip(int) behave like those of class InputStream (section 21.8).

- int available() returns the number of bytes that can be read or skipped without blocking.
- void close() closes the stream, as in InputStream.
- int read() reads one byte, as in InputStream.
- int read(byte[] b) reads bytes into b, as in InputStream.
- int read(byte[] b, int i, int n) reads into b[i..(i+n-1)], as in InputStream.
- Object readObject() reads, deserializes, and returns an object, which must have been previously serialized. Throws ClassNotFoundException if the declaration (class file) for an object that is being deserialized cannot be found. Throws ObjectStreamException or one of its subclasses if no object can be read from the stream, e.g., if end-of-stream is encountered before the object is complete.
- long skip(long n) skips n bytes, as in InputStream.

The interface ObjectOutput has all the methods of interface DataOutput (section 21.10) and the following one. Class ObjectOutputStream implements ObjectOutput.

- void writeObject(Object obj) writes the object using serialization. All classes being serialized must implement the Serializable interface; otherwise NotSerializableException is thrown.

Interface Externalizable is a subinterface of Serializable that can be implemented by classes that need full control over the serialization and deserialization of their objects.

Example 107 Serialization to the Same ObjectOutputStream Preserves Sharing

Objects o1 and o2 refer to a shared object c of class SC. We serialize o1 and o2 to the same file using a single ObjectOutputStream, so we get a single copy of the shared object. When we deserialize the objects and bind them to variables o1i and o2i, we also get a single copy of the shared SC object:

```
class SC implements Serializable { int ci; }
class SO implements Serializable {
  int i; SC c;
  SO(int i, SC c) { this.i = i; this.c = c; }
  void cprint() { System.out.print("i" + i + "c" + c.ci + " "); }
}
...
File f = new File("objects.dat");
// Create the objects and write them to file.
SC c = new SC();
SO o1 = new SO(1, c), o2 = new SO(2, c);
o1.c.ci = 3; o2.c.ci = 4;                    // Update the shared c twice
o1.cprint(); o2.cprint();                    // Prints: i1c4 i2c4
OutputStream os = new FileOutputStream(f);
ObjectOutputStream oos = new ObjectOutputStream(os);
oos.writeObject(o1); oos.writeObject(o2); oos.close();
// Read the objects from file.
InputStream is = new FileInputStream(f);
ObjectInputStream ois = new ObjectInputStream(is);
SO o1i = (SO)(ois.readObject()), o2i = (SO)(ois.readObject());
o1i.cprint(); o2i.cprint();                  // Prints: i1c4 i2c4
o1i.c.ci = 5; o2i.c.ci = 6;                  // Update the shared c twice
o1i.cprint(); o2i.cprint();                  // Prints: i1c6 i2c6
```

Example 108 Serialization to Distinct ObjectOutputStreams Does Not Preserve Sharing

If we serialize the objects o1 and o2 from example 107 to the same file using two different ObjectOutput-Streams, each object stream will write a copy of the shared object. When we deserialize the objects, we get two copies of the previously shared SC object:

```
// Create the objects (as in above example) and write them to file.
ObjectOutputStream oos1 = new ObjectOutputStream(os);
oos1.writeObject(o1); oos1.flush();
ObjectOutputStream oos2 = new ObjectOutputStream(os);
oos2.writeObject(o2); oos2.close();
// Read the objects from file, nonshared c.
InputStream is = new FileInputStream(f);
ObjectInputStream ois1 = new ObjectInputStream(is);
SO o1i = (SO)(ois1.readObject());
ObjectInputStream ois2 = new ObjectInputStream(is);
SO o2i = (SO)(ois2.readObject());
o1i.cprint(); o2i.cprint();                  // Prints: i1c4 i2c4
o1i.c.ci = 5; o2i.c.ci = 6;                  // Update two different c's
o1i.cprint(); o2i.cprint();                  // Prints: i1c5 i2c6
```

21.12   Buffered Input and Output

Writing one byte or character at a time to a file or network connection is very inefficient. It is better to collect the bytes or characters in a buffer, and then write the whole buffer in one operation. The same holds for reading from a file or network connection. However, buffering will not speed up input from and output to byte arrays, character arrays, strings, or string buffers.

To buffer a plain input stream is, create a BufferedInputStream from is and read from that stream instead; and similarly for output streams, readers, and writers.

The operation flush() can be used on a buffered stream to request that the output actually gets written to the underlying stream. A buffered stream should be properly closed by a call to close() to ensure that all data written to the buffer are eventually written to the underlying stream.

Class BufferedReader has all the methods of class Reader (section 21.4) and these constructors and method:

- BufferedReader(Reader rd) creates a buffered reader that reads from rd.
- BufferedReader(Reader rd, int sz) creates a buffered reader with buffer of size sz. It throws IllegalArgumentException if sz <= 0.
- String readLine() reads a line of text. A line is terminated by line feed ("\n") or carriage return ("\r") or carriage return and line feed ("\r\n"). Returns the line without any line termination characters; returns null at end-of-stream.

Class BufferedWriter has all the methods of Writer (section 21.5) and also these constructors and method:

- BufferedWriter(Writer wr) creates a buffered writer that writes to stream wr.
- BufferedWriter(Writer wr, int sz) creates a buffered writer with a buffer of size sz. It throws IllegalArgumentException if sz <= 0.
- void newLine() writes a line separator, such as "\n" or "\r\n", depending on the platform.

Class BufferedInputStream is a subclass of FilterInputStream. It has the same methods as InputStream (section 21.8) and these constructors:

- BufferedInputStream(InputStream is) creates a BufferedInputStream that reads from stream is.
- BufferedInputStream(InputStream is, int sz) creates a BufferedInputStream with buffer size sz; throws IllegalArgumentException if sz <= 0.

Class BufferedOutputStream is a subclass of FilterOutputStream. It has the same methods as OutputStream (section 21.9) and these constructors:

- BufferedOutputStream(OutputStream os) creates a BufferedOutputStream that writes to stream os.
- BufferedOutputStream(OutputStream os, int sz) creates a BufferedOutputStream with a buffer of size sz; throws IllegalArgumentException if sz <= 0.

Example 109 Output Buffering

Buffering may speed up writes to a FileOutputStream by a large factor. Buffering the writes to a FileWriter has less effect, because a FileWriter is an OutputStreamWriter, which buffers the bytes converted from written characters before writing them to an underlying FileOutputStream. In one experiment, buffering made writes to a FileOutputStream 18 times faster and writes to a FileWriter only two or three times faster.

```
public static void main(String[] args) throws IOException {
  OutputStream os1 = new FileOutputStream("tmp1.dat");
  writeints("Unbuffered: ", 1000000, os1);
  OutputStream os2 = new BufferedOutputStream(new FileOutputStream("tmp2.dat"));
  writeints("Buffered:   ", 1000000, os2);
  Writer wr1 = new FileWriter("tmp1.dat");
  writeints("Unbuffered: ", 1000000, wr1);
  Writer wr2 = new BufferedWriter(new FileWriter("tmp2.dat"));
  writeints("Buffered:   ", 1000000, wr2);
}

static void writeints(String msg, int count, OutputStream os) throws IOException {
  Timer t = new Timer();
  for (int i=0; i<count; i++)
    os.write(i & 255);
  os.close();
  System.out.println(msg + t.check());
}

static void writeints(String msg, int count, Writer os) throws IOException {
  Timer t = new Timer();
  for (int i=0; i<count; i++)
    os.write(i & 255);
  os.close();
  System.out.println(msg + t.check());
}
```

For efficiency, one should usually wrap buffered streams around file streams and socket streams as follows:

Replace	By
new FileInputStream(e)	new BufferedInputStream(new FileInputStream(e))
new FileOutputStream(e)	new BufferedOutputStream(new FileOutputStream(e))
new FileWriter(e)	new BufferedWriter(new FileWriter(e))
new FileReader(e)	new BufferedReader(new FileReader(e))

21.13   Random Access Files: RandomAccessFile

Class RandomAccessFile is used for input from and output to so-called *random access files*. The data in a random access file can be accessed in any order, in contrast to streams, which can be read and written only sequentially from the beginning. Thus a random access file is similar to an extensible byte array stored on the file system. A random access file has an associated file pointer, which determines where the next read or write operation will begin. Setting the file pointer permits random access to all parts of the file (albeit thousands or millions times more slowly than to a byte array stored in memory). The file pointer is an offset from the beginning of the file; the first byte in the file has offset 0, the last byte in a file raf has offset raf.length()-1. The method call seek(pos) sets the file pointer to point at byte number pos.

Class RandomAccessFile implements the DataInput and DataOutput interfaces (section 21.10) and has the following constructors and additional methods. The methods read(), read(byte[]), and read(byte[], int, int) behave as in InputStream (section 21.8); in particular, they return −1 on end-of-file, and block until at least one byte of input is available. The methods readt(), where t is a type, behave as in DataInput (section 21.10); in particular, they throw EOFException on end-of-file.

- RandomAccessFile(String name, String mode) creates a new random access file stream and associates it with a file of the given name on the file system. Initially the file pointer is at offset 0. Throws IOException if the name indicates a directory. The mode must be "r" for read-only, or "rw" for read-write; otherwise IllegalArgumentException is thrown. If the file does not exist on the file system, and the mode is "r", then FileNotFoundException is thrown, but if the mode is "rw", then a new empty file is created if possible. If the mode is "r", any call to the write methods will throw IOException.

- RandomAccessFile(File file, String mode) works like the preceding, but associates the random access file stream with file.

- void close() closes the file stream.

- FileDescriptor getFD() returns the file descriptor associated with the stream.

- long getFilePointer() returns the current value of the file pointer.

- long length() returns the length of the file in bytes.

- int read() reads one byte, as in InputStream.

- int read(byte[] b) reads into array b, as in InputStream.

- int read(byte[] b, int i, int n) reads at most n bytes into b, as in InputStream.

- void seek(long pos) sets the file pointer to byte number pos. Throws IOException if pos<0. The file pointer may be set beyond end-of-file; a subsequent write will then extend the file's length.

- void setLength(long newlen) sets the length of the file by truncating or extending it (at the end); in the case of extension, the content of the extension is undefined.

Example 110 Organizing a String Array File for Random Access

This example shows a way to implement random access to large numbers of texts, such as millions of cached Web pages or millions of DNA sequences. We define a string array file to have three parts: (1) a sequence of Strings, each of which is in Java modified UTF-8 format; (2) a sequence of long integers, representing the start offsets of the strings; and (3) an integer, which is the number of strings in the file. (Note that Java limits the length of each UTF-encoded string; using a slightly more complicated representation in the file, we could lift this restriction.)

By putting the number of strings and the string offset table at the end of the file rather than at the beginning, we do not need to know the number of strings or the length of each string before writing the file. The strings can be written to the file incrementally, and the only structure we need to keep in memory is the table (ArrayList) of string lengths.

```
static void writeStrings(String filename, Iterator strIter)
  throws IOException {
  RandomAccessFile raf = new RandomAccessFile(filename, "rw");
  raf.setLength(0);                                    // Truncate the file
  ArrayList offsettable = new ArrayList();             // Contains Longs
  while (strIter.hasNext()) {
    offsettable.add(new Long(raf.getFilePointer()));   // Store string offset
    raf.writeUTF((String)strIter.next());              // Write string
  }
  Iterator iter = offsettable.iterator();
  while (iter.hasNext())                               // Write string offsets
    raf.writeLong(((Long)iter.next()).longValue());
  raf.writeInt(offsettable.size());                    // Write string count
  raf.close();
}
```

Example 111 Random Access Reads from a String Array File

The method call readOneString(f, i) reads string number i from a string array file f (example 110) in three stages, using three calls to seek. First, it reads the offset table length N from the last 4 bytes of the file. Second, since an int takes 4 bytes and a long takes 8 bytes (section 5.1), the string offset table must begin at position length()-4-8*N, and so the offset si of string number i can be read from position length()-4-8*N+8*i. Third, the string itself is read from offset si.

```
static String readOneString(String filename, int i) throws IOException {
  final int INTSIZE = 4, LONGSIZE = 8;
  RandomAccessFile raf = new RandomAccessFile(filename, "r");
  raf.seek(raf.length() - INTSIZE);
  int N = raf.readInt();
  raf.seek(raf.length() - INTSIZE - LONGSIZE * N + LONGSIZE * i);
  long si = raf.readLong();
  raf.seek(si);
  String s = raf.readUTF();
  raf.close();
  return s;
}
```

21.14   Files, Directories, and File Descriptors

21.14.1   Path Names in a File System: Class File

An object of class File represents a path name, that is, a directory/file path in the file system. The path name may denote a directory, a data file, or nothing at all (if there is no file or directory of that name). Even if the path name denotes a file or directory, a given program may lack the permission to read or write that file or directory. These are a few of the constructors and methods in class File:

- File(String pname) creates a path name corresponding to the string pname.
- boolean exists() returns true if a file or directory denoted by this path name exists.
- String getName() returns this path name as a string.
- boolean isDirectory() tests whether the file denoted by this path name is a directory.
- boolean isFile() tests whether the file denoted by this path name is a normal file.
- long length() returns the length of the file in bytes, or 0 if the file does not exist.
- File[] listFiles() returns the files and directories in the directory denoted by the path name; returns null on error or if the path name does not denote a directory.
- boolean mkdir() creates the directory named by this path name.

21.14.2   File System Objects: Class FileDescriptor

An object of class FileDescriptor is a file descriptor, an internal representation of an active file system object, such as an open file or an open socket. A file descriptor may be obtained from a FileInputStream (section 21.8) or FileOutputStream (section 21.9). The class has this method:

- void sync() requests that all system buffers are synchronized with the underlying physical devices; blocks until this has been done. Throws SyncFailedException if it cannot be done.

The class has static fields in, out, and err, which are the file descriptors associated with the standard input (System.in), standard output (System.out), and standard error (System.err) streams.

21.15   Thread Communication: PipedInputStream and PipedOutputStream

Threads (chapter 15) execute concurrently and may communicate asynchronously using internal pipes. A *pipe* is a pair of a PipedInputStream and a PipedOutputStream, or a pair of a PipedReader and a PipedWriter. By contrast, communication with other processes or with remote computers uses InputStreams and OutputStreams, possibly obtained from operating system sockets, briefly described in section 21.16.

To create a pipe, create one end of it by outpipe = new PipedOutputStream(), then use that to create and connect the other end by inpipe = new PipedInputStream(outpipe). Either end may be created first. A pipe end can be connected only once.

A producer thread writes to a PipedOutputStream (or PipedWriter), and a consumer thread reads from a PipedInputStream (or PipedReader) associated with the PipedOutputStream (or PipedWriter). If the producer thread is fast and the pipe fills up, then the next write operation blocks until there is room for data in the pipe. If the consumer thread is fast and there are no available data in the pipe, then the next read operation blocks until data become available. When either the consumer or the producer dies, and one end of the pipe is destroyed, the next write (or read) at the other end of the pipe throws an IOException.

Example 112 Reading and Printing a Directory Hierarchy

The call showDir(0, pathname) will print the path name, and if the path name exists and is a directory, then showDir recursively prints all its subdirectories and files. Because indent is increased for every recursive call, the layout reflects the directory structure.

```
static void showDir(int indent, File file) throws IOException {
  for (int i=0; i<indent; i++)
    System.out.print('-');
  System.out.println(file.getName());
  if (file.isDirectory()) {
    File[] files = file.listFiles();
    for (int i=0; i<files.length; i++)
      showDir(indent+4, files[i]);
  }
}
```

Example 113 Internal Pipes Between Threads

The producer thread writes the infinite sequence of prime numbers $2, 3, 5, 7, 11, 13, \ldots$ to a PipedOutputStream, while the consumer (the main thread) reads from a PipedInputStream connected to the PipedOutputStream. Actually, the producer writes to a DataInputStream built on top of the PipedOutputStream, and the consumer reads from a DataInputStream built on top of the PipedInputStream, because we want to send integers, not only bytes, through the pipe.

```
PipedOutputStream outpipe = new PipedOutputStream();
PipedInputStream inpipe = new PipedInputStream(outpipe);
final DataOutputStream outds = new DataOutputStream(outpipe);
DataInputStream inds = new DataInputStream(inpipe);
// This thread outputs primes to outds -> outpipe -> inpipe -> inds:
class Producer extends Thread {
  public void run() {
    try {
      outds.writeInt(2);
      for (int p=3; true; p+=2) {
        int q=3;
        while (q*q <= p && p%q != 0)
          q+=2;
        if (q*q > p)
          { outds.writeInt(p); System.out.print("."); }
      }
    } catch (IOException e) { System.out.println("<terminated>: " + e); }
  }
}

new Producer().start();
for (;;) {                              // Forever
  for (int n=0; n<10; n++)              //   output 10 primes
    System.out.print(inds.readInt() + " ");   //   and
  System.in.read();                     //   wait for Enter
}
```

21.16   Socket Communication

Whereas a pair of Java threads can communicate through a local pipe (e.g., PipedInputStream), a pair of distinct processes may communicate through *sockets*. The processes may be on the same machine, or on different machines connected by a network.

Sockets are often used in client/server architectures, where the server process creates a *server socket* that listens for connections from clients. When a client connects to the server socket, a fresh socket is created on the server side and is connected to the socket that the client used when connecting to the server. The socket connection is used for bidirectional communication between client and server; both ends can obtain an input stream and an output stream from the socket.

Here are a constructor and some methods from the ServerSocket class in package java.net:

- ServerSocket(int port) creates a server socket on the given port.
- Socket accept() listens for a connection, blocking until a connection is made. Creates and returns a new Socket when a connection is made. If a timeout is set, the call to accept throws InterruptedIOException when the timeout expires.
- void close() closes the server socket.
- void setSoTimeout(int tmo) sets the timeout so that a call to accept will time out after tmo milliseconds, if positive. Disables timeout (the default) if tmo is zero.

Here are a constructor and some methods from the Socket class in package java.net:

- Socket(String host, int port) creates a client socket and connects to a given port on the given host. The host may be a name ("localhost") or an IP address ("127.0.0.1").
- void close() closes the socket.
- InetAddress getInetAddress() returns the address to which this socket is connected, as an object of class java.net.InetAddress; methods getHostName() and getHostAddress() can be used to convert this address to a string.
- InputStream getInputStream() returns the input stream associated with this socket.
- OutputStream getOutputStream() returns the output stream associated with this socket.
- void setSoTimeout(int tmo) sets the timeout so that a call to read on the input stream obtained from this socket will time out after tmo milliseconds, if positive. If tmo is zero, then timeout is disabled (the default). If a timeout is set, a call to read throws InterruptedIOException when the timeout expires.

The Socket and ServerSocket classes are declared in the Java class library package java.net. The Java class library documentation [3] provides more information about sockets and server sockets.

Example 114 Socket Communication Between Processes

This example program runs as a server process or as a client process, depending on the first command line argument. The server and client may run on the same machine, or on different machines communicating via a network. Several clients may connect to the same server. The server creates a server socket that accepts connections on port 2357. When a client connects, a new client socket is created and an integer is received on that socket. If the integer is a prime, the server replies `true` on the same socket, otherwise `false`.

Each client process asks the server about the primality of the numbers 1 through 999 and prints those that are primes.

It is rather inefficient for the client to create a new socket for every request to the server, but it suffices for this example. Also, buffering the input and output streams may speed up socket communication (section 21.12).

```
import java.io.*;
import java.net.*;

class SocketTest {
  final static int PORT = 2357;

  public static void main(String[] args) throws IOException {
    boolean server = args.length == 1 && args[0].equals("server");
    boolean client = args.length == 2 && args[0].equals("client");
    if (server) {                // Server: accept questions about primality
      ServerSocket serversock = new ServerSocket(PORT);
      for (;;) {
        Socket sock = serversock.accept();
        DataInputStream dis  = new DataInputStream(sock.getInputStream());
        DataOutputStream dos = new DataOutputStream(sock.getOutputStream());
        int query = dis.readInt();
        dos.writeBoolean(isprime(query));
        dis.close(); dos.close();
      }
    } else if (client) {         // Client: ask questions about primality
      for (int i=1; i<1000; i++) {
        Socket sock = new Socket(args[1], PORT);
        DataOutputStream dos = new DataOutputStream(sock.getOutputStream());
        DataInputStream dis = new DataInputStream(sock.getInputStream());
        dos.writeInt(i);
        if (dis.readBoolean())
          System.out.print(i + " ");
        dos.close(); dis.close();
      }
    } else { ... }               // Neither server nor client
  }

  static boolean isprime(int p) { ... return true if p is prime ... }
}
```

References

[1] The authoritative reference on the Java programming language is J. Gosling, B. Joy, G. Steele, and G. Bracha, *The Java Language Specification*, 2nd ed. (Boston: Addison Wesley, 2000). Browse or download in HTML (573 KB) at <http://java.sun.com/docs/books/jls/>.

[2] An introduction to all aspects of Java programming is K. Arnold, J. Gosling, and D. Holmes, *The Java Programming Language*, 3rd ed. (Boston: Addison Wesley, 2000).

[3] The Java class libraries (or Java Core API) are described in two volumes of *The Java Class Libraries, Second Edition* (Boston: Addison Wesley, 1997/98). Volume 1, by P. Chan, R. Lee, and D. Kramer, covers `java.io`, `java.lang`, `java.math`, `java.net`, `java.text`, and `java.util`. Volume 2, by P. Chan and R. Lee, covers `java.applet`, `java.awt`, and `java.beans`. Also available is P. Chan, R.Lee, and D. Kramer, *The Java Class Libraries: 1.2 Supplement* (Boston: Addison Wesley, 1999).

The class library documentation can be downloaded (22 MB) at <http://java.sun.com/docs/> or browsed at <http://java.sun.com/j2se/1.4/docs/api/>.

[4] A compact guide to Java programming style is *The Elements of Java Style* (Cambridge: Cambridge University Press, 2000) by A. Vermeulen *et al*.

[5] The Unicode character encoding (<http://www.unicode.org/>) corresponds to part of the Universal Character Set (UCS), which is international standard ISO 10646-1:2000. The UTF-8 is a variable-length encoding of UCS, in which seven-bit ASCII characters are encoded as themselves, described in Annex R of this standard.

[6] Floating-point arithmetic is described in the ANSI/IEEE Standard for Binary Floating-Point Arithmetic (IEEE Std 754-1985).

Index

! (logical negation), 29
!= (not equal to), 29
% (remainder), 29
& (bitwise and), 29, 30
& (logical strict and), 29, 30
&& (logical and), 29, 30
* (multiplication), 29
+ (addition), 29
+ (string concatenation), 8, 29
++ (increment), 29
+= (compound assignment), 29
- (minus sign), 29
- (subtraction), 29
-- (decrement), 29
/ (division), 29
; (semicolon), 41
    misplaced (example), 45
< (less than), 29
<< (left shift), 29, 30
<= (less than or equal to), 29
= (assignment), 29
== (equal to), 29, 30
> (greater than), 29
>= (greater than or equal to), 29
>> (signed right shift), 29, 30
>>> (unsigned right shift), 29, 30
?: (conditional expression), 29, 32
^ (bitwise exclusive-or), 29, 30
^ (logical strict exclusive-or), 29, 30
| (bitwise or), 29, 30
| (logical strict or), 29, 30
|| (logical or), 29, 30
~ (bitwise complement), 29, 30

abs method (Math), 64
absolute value (example), 33, 43
abstract
    class, 16
    method, 20
accept method (net), 104
access modifiers, 18
accessible
    class, 16

    member, 18
    method, 38
acos method (Math), 64
actual parameter, 36
actual-list, 36
add method (collection), 70–72
addAll method (collection), 70–72
addFirst method (collection), 71
addition operator (+), 29
addLast method (collection), 71
ambiguous method call, 21, 38, 39
amortized complexity, 80
AnimatedCanvas class (example), 61
anonymous local class, 24
append method (StringBuffer), 66
applicable method, 38
args (command line arguments), 62
argument, 36
    concatenation (example), 9, 67
arithmetic operators, 30
ArithmeticException, 30, 54
array, 10–13
    access, 10
    assignment to element, 10
    assignment type check, 10
    creation, 10
    element, 10
    element type, 10
    index, 10
    initializer, 10
    jagged, 13
    multidimensional, 12
    rectangular, 13
    type, 4, 10
array product (example), 33, 47
ArrayIndexOutOfBoundsException, 10, 54
ArrayList class (collection), 68, 71
Arrays class (collection), 12
ArrayStoreException, 10, 54
ASCII character encoding, 8
asin method (Math), 64
asList method (Arrays), 12, 79
assert statement, 50

AssertionError, 50, 54
assignment
    array element, 10
    compound, 29, 32
    expression, 32
    operators (=, +=, ...), 32
    statement, 41
associativity, 28, 29
atan method (Math), 64
atan2 method (Math), 64
available method (io), 92, 96

Bank class (example), 59
binary input-output, 94
binarySearch method (Arrays), 12, 79
binarySearch method (collection), 78
bit, 4
bitwise and operator (&), 29
bitwise complement operator (~), 29
bitwise exclusive-or operator (^), 29
bitwise or operator (|), 29
block (io), 84
block-statement, 41
boolean (primitive type), 4, 40
Boolean class (wrapper), 4
break statement, 46
buffer
    example, 61, 99
    input, 98
    output, 98
    streams, 99
    string, 66–67
Buffer class (example), 61
BufferedInputStream class (io), 98
BufferedReader class (io), 91, 98
BufferedWriter class (io), 98
byte, 4
byte (primitive type), 4, 40
Byte class (wrapper), 4
byte stream, 82

C.class (Class object for C), 58
C.super.m (method in superclass of enclosing class),
    36
C.this (enclosing object reference), 24, 26
call-by-value, 36

case, 42
cast. *See* type cast
catch, 48
catching an exception, 48
ceil method (Math), 64
char (primitive type), 4, 40
character
    counting (example), 9
    escape sequence, 8
    replacing by character (example), 11
    replacing by string (example), 67
    stream, 82
Character class (wrapper), 4
charAt method (String), 8
charAt method (StringBuffer), 66
CharConversionException, 54
checked exception, 54
checkError method (io), 88
class, 14–25
    abstract, 16
    anonymous local, 24
    body, 14
    declaration, 14
    file, 2, 62
    final, 16
    hierarchy, 16
    inner, 14, 24, 32
    libraries, 106
    loading, 2, 22, 26
    local, 14, 24, 62
    member, 14
    modifier, 14
    name, 14, 62
    nested, 14, 24, 62
    of an object, 26, 28, 32
    public, 16, 62
    subclass, 16
    top-level, 14
    versus type, 28
    wrapper, 4
Class class, 58
class-body, 14
class-declaration, 14, 52
class-modifier, 14
ClassCastException, 40, 54
ClassNotFoundException, 54, 96

`clear` method (collection), 70
`clear` method (map), 73
`close` method (io), 84, 86, 87, 92, 93, 96, 98, 100
`close` method (net), 104
codons (example), 13
collection
  classes, 68–81
  synchronized, 70
  traversing (example), 77
  unmodifiable, 70
  view of, 70
Collection interface (collection), 68, 70
Collections class (collection), 78
ColoredPoint class (example), 23, 53
command line arguments, 62
  example, 9, 67
comment, 2
`commentChar` method (io), 90
Comparable interface, 76
comparator (example), 79
Comparator interface (collection), 72, 74, 76
`comparator` method (collection), 72
`comparator` method (map), 74
`compare` method (Comparator), 76
`compareTo` method (Comparable), 72, 74, 76
`compareTo` method (String), 8
`compareToIgnoreCase` method (String), 8
comparison operators, 29
compatible types, 5
compilation, 2, 62
compile-time constant, 42
complexity
  amortized, 80
  time, 80
compound assignment, 29, 32
`concat` method (String), 8
concatenating arguments (example), 9, 67
concordance (example), 75, 77
concurrency, 56–61
ConcurrentModificationException, 54, 76
conditional expression, 32
constant. *See also* literal
  compile-time, 42
  named, 6
constructor
  body, 22

call, 32
  to superclass, 16
  declaration, 22
  default, 16, 22
  modifier, 22
  signature, 5, 22
constructor-declaration, 22
constructor-modifier, 22
`contains` method (collection), 70
`containsAll` method (collection), 70
`containsKey` method (map), 73
`containsValue` method (map), 73
`continue` statement, 46
conversion, 40
  narrowing, 40
  widening, 40
`copy` method (collection), 78
core API, 106
`cos` method (Math), 64
Created (thread state), 57
current object, 14, 34
`currentThread` method (Thread), 60

database query (example), 75
DataInput interface (io), 94
DataInputStream class (io), 92, 95
DataOutput interface (io), 94
DataOutputStream class (io), 93, 95
date book (example), 79
date checking (example), 3
Dead (thread state), 57
decimal integer literal, 4
DecimalFormat class, 88
declaration
  class, 14
  constructor, 22
  field, 18
  formal parameter, 20
  interface, 52
  method, 20
  variable, 6
decrement operator (`--`), 29, 30
default
  access, 18
  constructor, 16, 22
  initial value

of array element, 10
of field, 18
package, 62
`default` clause in switch, 42
`delete` method (StringBuffer), 66
deterministic finite automaton (example), 81
die (example), 11, 89
die frequencies (example), 11
directory hierarchy (example), 103
division
floating-point, 30
integer, 30
operator (/), 29
by zero, 30
`do-while` statement, 44
`double` (primitive type), 4, 40, 64
Double class (wrapper), 4
dynamic dispatch, 38
dynamically typed, 70

E constant (Math), 64
element
of array, 10
type, 10
`else`, 42
empty statement, 41
`-enableassertions` (option), 50
Enabled (thread state), 56, 57
enclosing object, 24, 26
end-of-stream, 84, 86, 90, 92, 94, 96, 98, 100
entry of map, 73
`entrySet` method (map), 73
Enumeration interface (collection), 76
`enumeration` method (collection), 78
EOFException, 54, 84, 94, 100
`eolIsSignificant` method (io), 90
equal to operator (==), 29
`equals` method (Arrays), 12
`equals` method (collection), 71, 72, 76
`equals` method (map), 73
`equals` method (String), 8
`equalsIgnoreCase` method (String), 8
Error (exception), 54
error status
of a PrintStream, 88
of a PrintWriter, 88

escape sequence, 8
exception, 54–55
catching, 48
checked, 54
class hierarchy (table), 54
example, 49
in static initializer, 22
throwing, 48
unchecked, 54
Exception, 54
ExceptionInInitializerError, 22, 54
execution, 2
`exists` method (io), 102
`exp` method (Math), 64
expression, 28–40
arithmetic, 30
array access, 10
array creation, 10
assignment, 32
conditional, 32
field access, 34
logical, 30
method call, 36–39
object creation, 32
statement, 41
type cast, 29, 40
type of, 28
extended signature, 5
extends-clause, 16, 52
Externalizable interface (io), 96

factorial (example), 65
field, 6, 18
access, 34
declaration, 18
description, 52
final, 18
initializer, 18
modifier, 18
shadowing, 6
static, 18
field initializer, 22
field-declaration, 18
field-desc-modifier, 52
field-description, 52
field-modifier, 18

file
    descriptor, 102
    jar, 62
    name (*see* path name)
    pointer, 100
    random access, 100
    sequential, 86, 87, 92, 93
    source, 62
File class (io), 102
FileDescriptor class (io), 102
FileInputStream class (io), 92, 97, 99
FileNotFoundException, 54, 86, 87, 92, 93, 100
FileOutputStream class (io), 93, 97, 99
FileReader class (io), 86, 91, 99
FileWriter class (io), 87, 89, 99
fill method (Arrays), 12
fill method (collection), 78
final
    class, 16
    field, 18
    method, 20
    parameter, 20
    variable, 6
finally, 48
first method (collection), 72
firstKey method (map), 74
float (primitive type), 4, 40, 64
Float class (wrapper), 4
floating-point
    division, 30
    literal, 4
    overflow, 30
    remainder, 30
floor method (Math), 64
flush method (io), 84, 87, 88, 93, 98
for statement, 44
formal parameter, 20
formal-list, 20

Gaussian random numbers (example), 65
get method (collection), 71
get method (map), 73
getEncoding method (io), 86, 87
getFD method (io), 92, 93, 100
getFilePointer method (io), 100
getFirst method (collection), 71

getInetAddress method (net), 104
getInputStream method (net), 104
getKey method (map), 73
getLast method (collection), 71
getLineNumber method (io), 91
getName method (io), 102
getOutputStream method (net), 104
getValue method (map), 73
greater than operator (>), 29
greater than or equal to operator (>=), 29

hashCode method (collection), 71, 72, 76
hashCode method (map), 73
HashMap class (map), 68, 73
HashSet class (collection), 68, 72
hasNext method (collection), 76
headMap method (map), 74
headSet method (collection), 72
hexadecimal integer literal, 4
HTML output (example), 89

IdentityHashMap class (map), 68, 73
IEEE754 floating-point standard, 4, 64, 106
IEEEremainder method (Math), 64
if statement, 42
if-else statement, 42
IllegalArgumentException, 54, 84, 98, 100
IllegalMonitorStateException, 54, 58
IllegalStateException, 54, 76
immediate superclass, 16
implements-clause, 52
import, 62
increment operator (++), 29, 30
index
    into array, 10
    into list (collection), 71
    into string, 8
indexOf method (collection), 71
IndexOutOfBoundsException, 54, 71, 78, 86, 87, 92, 93
initialization
    of nonstatic fields, 18, 22
    of static fields, 18
initializer, 22
    array, 10
    block, 22

nonstatic, 22
static, 22
field, 18, 22
variable, 6
initializer-block, 22
inner class, 14, 24, 32
inner object, 26
input, 82–105
input-output, 82–105
   buffering, 98–99
   byte stream, 92–97
   character stream, 86–91
   examples, 85
   random access, 100–101
   socket, 104–105
InputStream class (io), 92
InputStreamReader class (io), 86
`insert` method (StringBuffer), 66
instance, 18
instance member, 14
`instanceof`, 29, 32
`int` (primitive type), 4, 40
integer
   division, 30
   literal, 4
   overflow, 30
   remainder, 30
Integer class (wrapper), 4
integer square root (example), 51
interface, 52–53
   declaration, 52
   modifier, 52
   nested, 62
   public, 52, 62
   subinterface, 52
interface-declaration, 52
interface-modifier, 52
`interrupt` method (Thread), 60
`interrupted` method (Thread), 60
interrupted status (of thread), 60
InterruptedException, 54, 60
InterruptedIOException, 54, 104
intersection closure (example), 81
InvalidClassException, 54
invariant, 51
invocation of method. *See* method call

io. *See* input-output
IOException, 54, 84, 86, 88, 100, 102
`isDirectory` method (io), 102
`isEmpty` method (collection), 70
`isEmpty` method (map), 73
`isFile` method (io), 102
`isInterrupted` method (Thread), 60
iterator, 76
Iterator interface (collection), 76
Iterator interface (example), 25
`iterator` method (collection), 70

jagged array (example), 13
jar file, 62
`jar` program, 62
Java program, 62
`java.io` package, 82
`java.lang` package, 56, 62
`java.net` package, 104
`java.nio` package, 82
`java.sql` package, 75
`java.text` package, 88
`java.util` package, 12, 68
`join` method (Thread), 60
Joining (thread state), 56, 57

`keySet` method (map), 73

label, 46
labeled statement, 46
`last` method (collection), 72
`lastIndexOf` method (collection), 71
`lastKey` method (map), 74
layout of program, 2
leap year (example), 31
left shift operator (`<<`), 29
left-associative, 28
`length` field (array), 10
`length` method (io), 100, 102
`length` method (String), 8
`length` method (StringBuffer), 66
less than operator (`<`), 29
less than or equal to operator (`<=`), 29
line counting (example), 83
`lineno` method (io), 90, 91
LineNumberReader class (io), 91

LinkedHashMap class (map), 68, 73
LinkedHashSet class (collection), 68, 72
LinkedList class (collection), 68, 71
List interface (collection), 68, 71
`listFiles` method (io), 102
`listIterator` method (collection), 71
literal
    floating-point, 4
    integer, 4
    primitive type, 4
    string, 8
loading of class, 22, 26
local class, 14, 24, 62
lock, 58
Locking (thread state), 56, 57
`log` method (Math), 64
logical and operator (`&&`), 29
logical negation operator (`!`), 29
logical operators, 30
logical or operator (`||`), 29
logical strict and operator (`&`), 29
logical strict exclusive-or operator (`^`), 29
logical strict or operator (`|`), 29
`long` (primitive type), 4, 40
Long class (wrapper), 4
loop statement, 44–45

map
    classes, 73–75
    entry, 73
    interface, 73
    sorted, 74
Map interface (map), 68, 73
Map.Entry interface (map), 73
`mark` method (io), 86, 92
`markSupported` method (io), 86, 92
Math class, 64
mathematical functions, 64–65
`max` method (collection), 78
`max` method (Math), 64
member, 14
    instance, 14
    nonstatic, 14
    private, 18
    static, 14
member class, 14

    nonstatic, 24
    static, 24
method, 20
    abstract, 20
    accessible, 38
    applicable, 38
    body, 20
    call, 36–39
        ambiguous, 21, 38, 39
        signature, 36
        statement, 41
    declaration, 20
    description, 52
    final, 20
    invocation (*see* method call)
    modifier, 20
    nonstatic, 20
    overloading, 20
    overriding, 16
    signature, 5, 20
    static, 20
method-declaration, 20
method-description, 52
method-modifier, 20
`min` method (collection), 78
`min` method (Math), 64
`mkdir` method (io), 102
monitor, 58
more specific signature, 5
most specific signature, 5
multidimensional array, 12
multiple threads (example), 57, 59
multiplication operator (`*`), 29
mutual exclusion (example), 59

name
    class, 62
    legal, 2
    parameter, 20
    path, 102
    reserved, 2
    source file, 62
named constant, 6, 52
naming conventions, 2
`Nan` (not a number), 64
narrowing conversion, 40

natural ordering (compareTo), 76
nCopies method (collection), 78
negation operator (-), 29
NegativeArraySizeException, 10, 54
nested class, 14, 24, 62
nested interface, 62
new
    array creation, 10, 29
    object creation, 24, 29, 32
newLine method (io), 98
next method (collection), 76
nextToken method (io), 90
nonstatic
    code, 14, 34
    field, 18
    initializer block, 22
    member, 14
    member class, 24
    method, 20
NoSuchElementException, 54, 71, 72, 74, 76, 78
not equal to operator (!=), 29
notify method (Object), 60
notifyAll method (Object), 60
NotSerializableException, 54, 96
nucleotides (example), 13
null, 4, 6
NullPointerException, 8, 38, 48, 54, 58
Number class, 4
numeric type, 4

O notation, 80
o.new (inner object creation), 32
object, 18, 26–28
    creation expression, 32
    current, 14, 34
    enclosing, 24, 26
    initialization, 22
    inner, 26
    locked, 60
    outer (*see* object, enclosing)
Object class, 5, 8, 16, 60
ObjectInput interface (io), 96
ObjectInputStream class (io), 96
ObjectOutput interface (io), 96
ObjectOutputStream class (io), 96
ObjectStreamException, 54, 84, 96

octal integer literal, 4
ordinaryChars method (io), 90
outer object. *See* object, enclosing
OutOfMemoryError, 54
output, 82–105
OutputStream class (io), 93
OutputStreamWriter class (io), 87
overflow
    floating-point, 30
    integer, 30
overloading
    constructor, 22
    method, 20
overriding a method, 16

package, 62–63
    access, 18
    default, 62
    java.io, 82
    java.lang, 56, 62
    java.net, 104
    java.nio, 82
    java.sql, 75
    java.text, 88
    java.util, 12, 68
padding a string (example), 67, 89
parameter, 6
    actual, 36
    final, 20
    formal, 20
    modifier, 20
    name, 20
    passing, 33, 36
parameter-modifier, 20
parseNumbers method (io), 90
path name, 102
phone prefix codes (example), 43
PI constant (Math), 64
pipe, 102
PipedInputStream class (io), 102
PipedOutputStream class (io), 102
PipedReader class (io), 102
PipedWriter class (io), 102
Point class (example), 15, 23
postdecrement operator, 29, 30
postincrement operator, 29, 30

pow method (Math), 64
precedence, 28
predecrement operator, 29, 30
preincrement operator, 29, 30
prime number server (example), 105
prime numbers (example), 103
primitive type, 4
print method (io), 84, 88
println method (io), 84, 88
PrintStream class (io), 88
PrintWriter class (io), 88, 89
private member, 18
program
    layout, 2
    legal, 2
promotion type, 28
protected member, 18, 63
public
    class, 16, 52, 62
    interface, 52, 62
    member, 18
put method (map), 73
putAll method (map), 73

quoteChar method (io), 90

random access file, 100
    example, 95, 101
random method (Math), 64
RandomAccess interface (collection), 71
RandomAccessFile class (io), 95, 100
read method (io), 84, 86, 92, 96, 100
readBoolean method (io), 94
readByte method (io), 94
readChar method (io), 94
readDouble method (io), 94
Reader class (io), 86
readFloat method (io), 94
readFully method (io), 94
readInt method (io), 94
readLine method (io), 94, 98
readLong method (io), 94
readObject method (io), 84, 96
readShort method (io), 94
readUnsignedByte method (io), 94
readUnsignedShort method (io), 94

readUTF method (io), 92, 94
ready method (io), 86
rectangular array (example), 13
reference type, 4
remainder
    floating-point, 30, 64
    integer, 30
    operator (%), 29
remove method (collection), 70, 71, 76
remove method (map), 73
removeAll method (collection), 70
removeFirst method (collection), 71
removeLast method (collection), 71
renaming the states of a DFA (example), 81
replace method (StringBuffer), 66
replaceAll method (collection), 78
replacing character by character (example), 11
replacing character by string (example), 67
reserved name, 2
reset method (io), 86, 92
resetSyntax method (io), 90
retainAll method (collection), 70
return statement, 46
return type, 20
    void, 20
return-type, 20
reverse method (collection), 78
reverse method (StringBuffer), 66
reverseOrder method (collection), 78
right alignment (example), 67, 89
right shift operator
    signed (>>), 29
    unsigned (>>>), 29
right-associative, 28, 32
rint method (Math), 64
rotate method (collection), 78
round method (Math), 64
Runnable interface, 61
Running (thread state), 56, 57
RuntimeException, 54

scope, 6
    of field, 6, 14
    of label, 46
    of member, 14
    of parameter, 6, 20

of variable, 6
seek method (io), 100
semicolon, 41
    misplaced (example), 45
Serializable interface, 96
serialization, 96
server socket, 104
ServerSocket class (net), 104
Set interface (collection), 68, 72
set membership (example), 79
set method (collection), 71
setCharAt method (StringBuffer), 66
setLength method (io), 100
setLineNumber method (io), 91
setSoTimeout method (net), 104
shadowing a field, 6
shared state, 56
shift operators, 30
short (primitive type), 4, 40
Short class (wrapper), 4
shortcut evaluation, 30
shuffle method (collection), 78
signature, 5
    constructor, 22
    extended, 5
    method, 20
    method call, 36
    more specific, 5
    most specific, 5
    subsumption, 5
    target, 38
signed right shift operator (>>), 29
sin method (Math), 64
singleton method (collection), 78
singletonList method (collection), 78
singletonMap method (collection), 78
size method (collection), 70
size method (io), 93
size method (map), 73
skip method (io), 84, 86, 92
skipBytes method (io), 94
sleep method (Thread), 60
Sleeping (thread state), 56, 57
socket, 104
    server, 104
Socket class (net), 104

sort method (Arrays), 12
sort method (collection), 78
SortedMap interface (map), 68, 74
sortedness check (example), 9
SortedSet interface (collection), 68, 72
-source (option), 50
source file, 62
SPoint class (example), 15
sqrt method (Math), 64
square root (example), 51
StackOverflowError, 54
standard error, 88
standard input, 92
standard output, 88
start method (Thread), 60
state, 28, 41
    of thread, 56, 57
    shared, 56
statement, 41–51
    assignment, 41
    block, 41
    break, 46
    continue, 46
    do-while, 44
    empty, 41
    for, 44
    if, 42
    if-else, 42
    labeled, 46
    loop, 44–45
    method call, 41
    return, 46
    switch, 42
    synchronized, 58
    throw, 48
    try-catch-finally, 48, 55
    while, 44
static
    class, 52
    code, 14
    field, 18
    initializer block, 22
    member, 14
    member class, 24
    method, 20
stream, 82

byte, 82
    character, 82
    creating, 83
StreamTokenizer class (io), 90, 91
string, 8–9
    buffer, 66–67
    character escape sequence, 8
    comparison, 8, 30
    concatenation, 8, 29
    from character array (example), 11
    literal, 8
    padding (example), 67
string array file (example), 101
String class, 8
`String.valueOf` method, 8
StringBuffer class, 66
StringIndexOutOfBoundsException, 8, 54, 66, 87
subclass, 16
subinterface, 52
`subList` method (collection), 71
`subMap` method (map), 74
`subSet` method (collection), 72
substring test (example), 47
subsumption, 5
subtraction operator (-), 29
subtype, 5
summing a file (example), 91
summing lines of a file (example), 91
`super`
    superclass constructor call, 16
    superclass member access, 16
superclass, 16
    immediate, 16
supertype, 5
`swap` method (collection), 78
`switch` statement, 42
`sync` method (io), 102
SyncFailedException, 54, 102
synchronization, 58–61
synchronized collection, 70
`synchronized` method, 58
`synchronized` statement, 58
`synchronizedList` method (collection), 78
`System.err` (standard error), 88
`System.in` (standard input), 92
`System.out` (standard output), 88

`tailMap` method (map), 74
`tailSet` method (collection), 72
`tan` method (Math), 64
temperature conversion (example), 89
`this`
    constructor call, 22
    current object reference, 14, 34
thread, 56–61
    communication, 56, 102
    operations, 60
    shared state, 58
    state, 56, 57
    state transitions, 56, 57
Thread class, 56, 60
thread safety
    of collections, 70
    of input-output, 84
    of string buffers, 66
`throw` statement, 48
Throwable (exception), 48, 54
throwing an exception, 48
`throws`, 20
throws-clause, 20
time
    complexity, 80
    constant, 80
    linear, 80
    logarithmic, 80
`toArray` method (collection), 70
`toDegrees` method (Math), 64
top-level class, 14
`toRadians` method (Math), 64
`toString` method, 8, 9, 15, 54
`toString` method (StringBuffer), 66
`transient`, 96
traversing a collection (example), 77
TreeMap class (map), 68, 74
TreeSet class (collection), 68, 72
`try-catch-finally` statement, 48, 55
type, 4–5
    array, 4, 10
    compatible, 5
    conversion, 40
    numeric, 4
    primitive, 4
    reference, 4

versus class, 28
type cast
    expression, 29, 40
    for primitive types, 40
    for reference types, 40

unchecked exception, 54
Unicode character encoding, 106
Unicode character encoding, 8
Universal Character Set, 106
unmodifiable collection, 70
unmodifiableList method (collection), 78
unsigned right shift operator (>>>), 29
UnsupportedEncodingException, 54
UnsupportedOperationException, 54, 70, 76
UTF-8 format, 92, 94, 101, 106
UTFDataFormatException, 54

value, 6
valueOf method (String), 8
values method (map), 73
variable, 6
    declaration, 6
    final, 6
    initializer, 6
    modifier, 6
variable-declaration, 6
variable-modifier, 6
Vector class (collection), 71
vessels (example), 17, 63
view of collection, 70, 78
void return type, 20

wait method (Object), 60
wait set, 58
Waiting (thread state), 56, 57
weekday (example), 43, 45, 47, 49
WeekdayException (example), 55
while statement, 44
whitespaceChars method (io), 90
widening conversion, 40
word list (example), 51
wordChars method (io), 90
worklist algorithm (example), 81
wrapper class, 4
write method (io), 84, 87, 93, 94

writeBoolean method (io), 94
writeByte method (io), 94
writeBytes method (io), 94
writeChar method (io), 94
writeChars method (io), 94
writeDouble method (io), 94
writeFloat method (io), 94
writeInt method (io), 94
writeLong method (io), 94
writeObject method (io), 84, 96
Writer class (io), 87
writeShort method (io), 94
writeUTF method (io), 94

yield method (Thread), 60